3000 800026 00622
St. Louis Community College

WITHDRAWN

FV

 St. Louis Community College

Forest Park
Florissant Valley
Meramec

Instructional Resources
St. Louis, Missouri

Overachieving Parents
Underachieving Children

Overachieving Parents
Underachieving Children

*Working Together
to Help Your Child
Find Success*

Dorothy A. Bodenburg, M.F.C.C.

Lowell House
Los Angeles

Contemporary Books
Chicago

Library of Congress Cataloging-in-Publication Data
Bodenburg, Dorothy A.
    Overachieving parents, underachieving children :
working together to help your child find success / Dorothy A.
Bodenburg.
        p. cm.
    Includes bibliographical references and index.
    ISBN 0-929923-57-X
    1. Parent and child—United States.   2. Underachiev-
ment—United States. 3. Parenting—United States. I. Title.
HQ755.85.B63   1992
649'.1—dc20   92-14570
                                                                        CIP

Copyright © 1992 by Dorothy A. Bodenburg, M.F.C.C., and
RGA Publishing Group, Inc. All rights reserved. No part of
this work may be reproduced or transmitted in any form or
by any means, electronic or mechanical, including photo-
copying and recording, or by any information storage or
retrieval system, except as may be expressly permitted by
the 1976 Copyright Act or in writing by the publisher.

Requests for such permissions should be addressed to:
        Lowell House
        2029 Century Park East, Suite 3290
        Los Angeles, CA 90067
        Publisher: Jack Artenstein
        Executive Vice-President: Nick Clemente
        Vice-President/Editor-in-Chief: Janice Gallagher
        Design: Nancy Freeborn

Manufactured in the United States of America

10 9 8 7 6 5 4 3 2 1

To the children of the world in their quest to be.

Table of Contents

Table of Contents

Acknowledgments

My deep respect and heartfelt gratitude go to the following people:

John and Vinnerella Bodenburg, my parents, who taught me that there are no limitations.

John Myers, my husband, who encouraged me with his consistent faith in my abilities and his love. His quest for self-actualization is an inspiration to me.

Janice Gallagher, Lowell House Editor-in-Chief, who gave me this opportunity, and Susan Golant, my editor, for her support and help.

Janet McClure and Vywamus, whose spirit will always be with me.

Marla Lipsky, Magdalen Daniels, Robyn Lawson, and Ron Bieler, for their encouragement.

To all my clients, former students, and people who have attended my various workshops, for allowing me to touch their lives and in turn touching mine.

Introduction

The underachieving child is like the slightly tarnished spoon in your silver drawer. You know it's just as precious as all the rest, but when you notice its dull patina you tend to reach for the bright spoon instead. As parents, we cannot afford to allow our children to continue to feel tarnished. If we do, they never bask in the shine of their own light and worth. Rather, we must understand how they began to tarnish in the first place, and how we let it happen.

As a teacher, school counselor, seminar leader for parenting programs, and a marriage, family, and child counselor, I have heard from hundreds of parents about their frustration with their children's underachievement. They have shared sincere, heart-rending stories of confusion, anger, disappointment, guilt, and sadness in themselves and their children.

Especially frustrated were the successful parents who "had it all"—important jobs, confidence in themsleves—in other words, the go-getters of life. These parents didn't understand how their children could be so different from themselves. In an attempt to help, they either became so frustrated that they exacerbated the situation or tried parenting strategies that backfired.

What these parents didn't recognize was that the interpersonal dynamics between overachieving parents and underachieving children were the cause of the problem. As a successful adult you have many goals. It's perfectly acceptable to feel busy and fulfilled by these goals. The difficulty occurs, however, when excessive desires for achievement for yourself and your child—overachieving attitudes—prevent you from understanding and recognizing who your child is. When you expect your youngster to conform to your vision of who you want him to be and he doesn't agree, trouble begins.

Everything you need to know to make your family and child successful, satisfied, and happy is in this book. These methods have helped hundreds of families before you.

Overachieving Parents

Underachieving Children

Part I

How Children Become Underachievers

Chapter One

Breaking the Cycle

I'm stuck!" Sharon lamented during a family therapy session in my office. "No matter what I do, I can't make Kenny finish his homework or complete simple chores around the house." Even though Sharon was a successful fabric designer, she felt like a failure as a parent.

I asked this overwrought mother to give me an example of her son's behavior. She sighed deeply. "He's always putting things off until the last minute. Every night when I come home from work, I ask him if his homework is done. Every night he mumbles as he continues to watch TV. Not until I start yelling will Kenny stomp into his room and return with his half-finished assignment. I make him redo most of it because it looks so sloppy."

Unfortunately, Kenny usually managed to manipulate his mom. Complaining that he couldn't accomplish everything she wanted, he successfully negotiated a reduction in his work load. Sharon's constant prodding and the ensuing tug of war not only caused tension and anger between mother and son, but also set a negative tone for the whole family. The continual anger Sharon felt toward her son caused her to be moody and irritable toward her husband.

Sharon was drained by these daily conflicts. What finally brought her to counseling, however, was the note sent home from Kenny's teacher explaining that he had lied about incomplete schoolwork. Lying was a behavior Sharon could neither tolerate nor understand. She already felt like a failure as a parent, but now she wondered whether something was seriously wrong with her son. Was Kenny to blame, or was she the problem?

Sharon isn't alone. In fact, hers is a problem I've seen hundreds of times in my family counseling practice.

Jack, a college professor, is shocked by his 11-year-old son's short attention span when he tries to help with homework. "Billy seems to get distracted by anything, even the dog walking in the room."

Elisa, a public relations executive, says her daughter does well for a while, but then always backslides. "Why does she do everything right sometimes and then all of a sudden stop working?"

Ralph's parents, who own a family restaurant, are constantly urging him to do something constructive instead of wasting time on what they consider to be unproductive activities such as watching TV, playing computer games, and listening to music. "How can he spend so many hours playing one computer game and still be unable to finish a half-hour math assignment?" they want to know.

In the Mackey family, frequent fights revolve around the same theme. When teenage son Richard doesn't get his way, he becomes sullen and combative. "He feels his life is totally his own, and we don't have any right to interfere. But he isn't taking any responsibility for himself, so what are we supposed to do?" wonders Mr. Mackey, a successful systems analyst.

The parents who come to see me complain that their children:

• are lazy, angry, moody, and critical of themselves and others
• lie to themselves and others about their responsibilities
• have difficulty planning for the future
• are disorganized
• have "selective" memories

- don't understand why they have to contribute to the family
- procrastinate and rebel
- resent criticism
- rationalize and hold unrealistic expectations
- are manipulative
- invent excuses

The litany of complaints goes on and on. On the other hand, kids complain that their overachieving parents are:

- controlling
- demanding
- critical
- inattentive
- preoccupied
- inconsistent
- angry and moody

Breaking the Cycle

As I talk with my clients, I see their frustration and disappointment with their underachieving children. They're mystified about what went wrong, and they feel helpless. Somehow their dreams of ideal parenting haven't materialized. They feel guilty when they see their children doing poorly, especially when they are unable to help them improve. As achieving individuals who are successful in their own lives, they can't understand why their parenting practices won't work. Underneath it all, they fear their children may be defective. How else to explain such irrational and unproductive behavior? "Is Bobby intellectually deficient?" they ask themselves. "Can he really do the work? How am I supposed to know?"

It's inevitable that having an underachieving child—a youngster who doesn't live up to his or her strengths and talents—causes you great concern. But you've probably found that most of the steps you take to try to correct the situation backfire. Because you don't understand what causes your child to be an underachiever, you don't know what to do to help, so you rely again and again on the same "tried-and-false" techniques. As a result, your child persists in underachieving behavior, and the cycle continues.

But here is the good news: In my experience, there is no such thing as underachieving children—only underachieving behaviors. I have worked with countless children and their families as a teacher, school counselor, and marriage and family therapist over the past 25 years. I have also dealt with these issues as a parent.

As a teacher, I worked with learning-disabled, average, and gifted children. Within each group of students there were those who underachieved. I structured the classroom environment so that I taught the skills and attitudes necessary for these students to succeed. When I was a school counselor, I worked with small groups of students to help them correct their faulty thinking, manage their feelings, and change specific behaviors that inhibited success. I offered parenting classes to teach the parents of these children specific skills that would change their youngsters' underachieving behaviors. In my private practice in Orange County, California, an area noted for overachievers, I have developed a model of a family system that supports the specific skills parents and children need in order to actualize the strengths and talents of all family members. Being part of two federal grants and one state grant on drug prevention afforded me the opportunity to research the causes of underachievement in children and design programs to help youngsters reach their potential.

The wonderful, hope-filled truth about all the underachieving children I have worked with is that their aptitudes, strengths, and talents are equal to those of their achieving peers. Under-achieving children are in no way defective or lacking in abilities or intellect. In fact, they have the ability to be top students and creative, successful individuals. Rather, it is the parent's perception that the child must meet certain expectations, and the child's perception that he or she can't meet these specific expectations, that cause the destructive family dynamic.

The first step toward breaking this cycle is to understand it.

The Dynamics of Over- and Underachievement

The behaviors of over- and underachievers may look different on the surface, but you may be surprised to learn that some of the attitudes are actually quite similar. By recognizing the similarities, you can identify with some of the causes underlying your child's underachieving behaviors.

Most likely, both you and your child tend to be influenced by other people's reactions. That's how you judge who you are. You may adopt as your own the expectations and standards of the people whose love or approval you want. This makes you feel secure that you will get the positive regard you need. But unfortunately, it can prevent you from developing your own yardstick for measuring yourself.

Moreover, when you become a parent, you want the people important to you to approve of your parenting. Since there is no one way to parent, you may believe that others' judgments of your parenting acumen depend upon your child's behavior. Is your child successful, personable, courteous, and all the other traits that comprise our perception of a "good" or achieving child? If she passes the test, then you are deemed a good parent. But if not, you feel disapproval or criticism. This can cause you to doubt your competency as a parent. You may even think, "If I can't produce a successful child, maybe I am doing something wrong," or, "Maybe there is something wrong with me."

Lacking an internal criterion for successful parenting that is independent of others' validation, you place yourself (and eventually your children) under pressure to continuously achieve.

Youngsters are sensitive. They see how important success is to you by the amount of time and energy you spend at work. They recognize your desire to achieve. Since they need your validation to understand who they are, they try to please you. That means trying on *your* behaviors. But how can they succeed when you convey the message that they must constantly try harder and do better? Once your child recognizes that he will never be "good enough," he may give up hope of pleasing you. He may develop underachieving behaviors as a protection against this harsh reality.

This tendency to seek external validation can make it more difficult for you and your child to feel safe to explore and form your own personalities and values. It allows other people—a boss, a mate, teachers, a friend—to influence what is important to you instead of your being comfortable with your own decisions. The skills in this book will help you develop your own concept of parenting, which will make you secure and confident in parenting practices. Your child will learn to perform at his own pace and in concert with his own talents.

What distinguishes the behavior of overachievers from that of underachievers is how they respond to external influences. Let's explore the difference.

Carla, age 42, came into therapy with her two teenage daughters, Tara, 15, and Kathy, 13, because of the recent death of her husband. Carla was feeling guilty about the intensity of her anger following her husband's death. She didn't know how to react to the variety of emotions and behaviors her girls were showing. Tara was an overachiever and Kathy was an underachiever, a common pattern in families. Their responses to this crisis demonstrate how over- and underachievers react to the desire and need for external validation.

Tara took cues from her mother, who was trying to keep their family life as normal as possible. Tara helped get dinner ready and took over many chores to ensure a regular schedule. Her feelings of insecurity were only quelled when she was in action and getting praise from her mom.

Kathy, on the other hand, withdrew from the family's collective uneasiness by becoming more involved with her friends. As a consequence, Carla was constantly reprimanding her for shirking her part. Kathy felt overwhelmed by new responsibilities that called for her to be more independent. She didn't have the skills or emotional maturity to be more responsible, so she withdrew, intensifying her feelings of worthlessness.

Overachievers embrace others' expectations as a way of guaranteeing validation. Underachievers resent having to live up to other's expectations because they know from experience that they can't measure up. Both fear that if they fail to win the approval of those important to them, they are unworthy.

Paradoxically, the need to feel worthy causes over- and underachievers to seek others' approval. But when people depend on others for validation, they become alienated from themselves and don't fully develop their unique strengths.

Over- and underachievers may also become fearful of taking risks. As an overachiever, one needs to specify the requirements for success in advance because public validation is important for one's confidence level. Failure or lack of clarity regarding goals can be emotionally distressing. Conversely, the underachiever fears risking any action that entails a specific competitive goal because risk increases the probability of public exposure and failure—something the underachieving child tries to avoid at all costs.

That's what happened to Samantha, a third-grader who was having a difficult time reading. Her parents, Henry and Marcia, felt driven to make sure Samantha knew how to read because they feared she would fall behind in school. Each day became a nightmare for the child because of the hours her parents made her practice reading drills and reading aloud to them. Samantha knew that learning to read was important to her parents. But she became angry and defensive during these help sessions because her parents made her feel like a failure.When Marcia corrected every mispronounced word, Samantha felt stupid. This feeling in turn caused her to feel angry at herself and her mother. She tried to hide whenever it was time for reading practice, to avoid her feelings of inadequacy and failure. Then, when Samantha learned that she was going to be in a special reading class, she threw a tantrum and was sent to her room.

During therapy, Samantha began to understand her anger. As we explored her behavior, Samantha realized she feared being in a special class because her teacher would recognize that she didn't know how to read. She worried that her teacher wouldn't like her, the same way she thought her mom didn't like her. "What if my friends call me names or don't like me anymore either?" she asked anxiously. Samantha just wanted to stay in the regular class and have everyone pretend she could read. For this eight-year-old, going into a special reading class was too much of a risk for her self-esteem.

Risk is difficult for underachievers as well as overachievers because failure is so painful. Both may lack the skills to change failure into a learning experience, so failure becomes a consequence to be avoided at all costs. This can stunt personal growth.

As an overachieving parent, you want your child to adopt your "try harder" attitude. Your life experiences have proven that this perspective works to support your desire to succeed. However, the pressure your child feels from this constant prodding to strive harder creates a fear in him that love is based on achievement. From his point of view, no matter what he does you still may not be satisfied. In fact, you may not be clear about your child's abilities. Therefore, you push him to go to the next level of competency to see if he can do it. Hence, he doesn't feel your love and approval. Underachieving behaviors are a signal that your child has given up the hope of receiving your love and approval.

From the skills taught in this book you will enjoy the process of getting to know your youngster's strengths and weaknesses. This recognition of who your child is will allow you to support and encourage your child in a way that is loving and positive.

How This Book Can Help

Over the past 25 years, I have worked with hundreds of families caught in the vicious overachieving/underachieving cycle. Trained as a teacher, school counselor, and marriage, family, and child therapist, I have helped families talk to each other, respect each other's strengths and weaknesses, and work together to help children find success. Many satisfied clients have asked me to write a book to help others. *Overachieving Parents/Underachieving Children* is a product of these requests. This book will teach you:

- how to express feelings and thoughts clearly and nonjudgmentally
- how to help your child set meaningful goals
- how to teach your youngster the skills necessary to achieve better grades
- how to develop a homework and household chore accountability system
- how to be objective about your child
- how to help your child cope with frustration, disappointment, and anger
- how to support your child in focusing on each of the many small steps necessary to achieve a goal
- how to make your child understand the relationship between responsibilities and privileges

- how to help your child trust his own life experiences
- how to help your child turn failure into a learning experience

Part I of *Overachieving Parents/Underachieving Children* covers the dynamics of over- and underachievement. Chapter 2 outlines seven reasons why youngsters find underachievement a useful, albeit frustrating, coping mechanism. Next, you'll find it helpful to recognize the innate differences between you and your child. Chapter 3 offers information on how disparate temperament and thinking styles can lead to parent-child conflict. Chapter 4 describes the different types of underachievers and shows you how to understand your child's behavior, thinking, and feelings. Chapter 5 explains how many well-intentioned parenting practices can actually create more problems than they solve.

In Part II, you'll learn strategies to help your child feel happy and successful within your family. Chapter 6 explains children's emotional needs. When you meet and understand your child's needs within the family, she will no longer feel like an outsider. This chapter helps you create a support structure that will facilitate your using the skills you'll learn in subsequent chapters. It provides you with a new family management system that supports and respects each individual.

Chapter 7 begins the practical program that lies at the heart of this book. This chapter gives plenty of exercises to improve family communication. Here you will learn the skill of attentive listening and how to respond without criticism. All of the skills presented are designed to help you communicate clearly while avoiding emotional triggers and incomplete reasoning.

Chapter 8 helps you and your youngster discover the specific skills he will need to succeed at the goals he sets for himself. You'll show your youngster how to analyze tasks and check for competence in each skill needed to achieve a goal, improve his grades, and take responsibility for his behavior. By using the suggestions and exercises in this chapter, you can guide your youngster toward becoming a top student.

Underachieving children can have special problems interacting with parents and other authority figures. In Chapter 9 you will learn what causes power struggles, how to observe your child objectively to understand what she needs from you, how to avoid getting your agenda mixed up with your child's, and how differences can be solved amiably.

Chapter 10 explores different attitudes toward failure and success. Suggestions on helping your child deal with discouragement, frustration, and anger are given along with tips for supporting your child's new behaviors. You will help your youngster enjoy the process of reaching goals instead of making the goals the ends in themselves.

How Thoughts and Feelings Impact Behavior

Throughout this book I will be using a concept that makes the process of changing behaviors easy to understand. It can be presented in a simple equation: thinking + feeling = action or behavior.

Thinking and feeling are inseparable. For every thought, there is a concomitant emotion attached. This is true whether or not you allow yourself to be aware of your feelings. And with every feeling, there is a thought that caused the emotional response. When your thinking and feeling are congruent, the action that follows supports you. But if thinking and feeling are at odds, you may behave in ways that don't support you. Through your thinking, you decide *what* you want to do. But before you act, it is important to check how you feel; feelings provide you with valuable information about yourself such as preferences, motivations, and limitations. Let's look at an example from my own life.

When I was 21, I became a stockbroker. The excitement I experienced at first waned quickly. But I didn't allow myself to feel a recurring sense of dissatisfaction. After all, I was doing well at my job. Yet getting up in the morning became increasingly difficult. When I finally asked myself how I felt about being a stockbroker, I learned that I was depressed. From my point of view, I wasn't making a difference in my life or in the lives of others. Moreover, there was not enough variety of activities to support my creativity. Each day was too much like the one that had preceded it. Eventually, I had to admit that this job wasn't for me. I was unhappy.

When I allowed myself to experience these feelings, I was able to think about the situation from a new perspective. I explored the financial ramifications of quitting. I realized that if I invested properly, I wouldn't have to give up my financial goals to do what I wanted. I thought about the value of being a teacher, remembering a teacher who had made a difference in my life. Whenever I thought about teaching, I immediately felt inspired and happy. Once my thinking and feelings were in alignment, it was easy to take the steps necessary to change careers.

Unfortunately, our society has misperceptions about feelings. They are often associated with weakness or instability. We fear that if we feel our emotions, we will become their victims, as if they have a life force all their own. So faulty thinking states that it is better to prevent oneself from feeling because it will only lead to problems. However, feelings are necessary and important. They help us defend, define, and expand who we are. Feelings and thoughts together comprise the human experience.

In this book, I will help you understand emotions so you can decide what you want to do with them. As you will see, feelings that are unrecognized or undealt with become a key factor in causing underachieving behaviors. The same is true of faulty or negative thinking.

As an overachieving parent, you want your child to be successful in all areas of life. You watch your child, assess how he is doing, and then react to his success or failure. But being overly focused on your child's achievements can rob you of a spontaneous, personal relationship with him. Getting to know him, being delighted in his growth, and watching his self-discovery are what bring joy to parenthood. I'll be sharing specific skills throughout this book to help you support your child in realizing his potential while enhancing family warmth and intimacy.

Chapter Two

Why Children Become Underachievers

As a successful person, you know how to reach lofty goals. You are capable of setting priorities, working hard, and delaying immediate gratification for long-term gains. You are responsible, organized, and efficient. In short, you get the job done! Most likely, you have accomplished some pretty remarkable things in your life and you want your child to do so, too. Yet children become underachievers for a variety of reasons. These include failure to live up to unrealistic ideals, escaping from responsibilities, balking at expectations, and crying out for help, attention, or love.

Although underachieving children may ask for their needs to be met in inappropriate ways, it is imperative to look at the messages behind their often unacceptable behaviors. These provide clues to the unmet needs and invisible pressures that lead to underachievement. Let's take a closer look at why children become underachievers.

Living Up to Unrealistic Ideals

When you see your child defy and oppose your expectations, you can't understand why anyone would engage in such self-destructive behaviors. Since you hope to be a role model for your youngster, it is natural for you to think he will easily pick up your habits, especially when achievement is part of your family's values. It becomes mystifying to you, therefore, when your child is an underachiever. You are not lazy or irresponsible, so how has he learned these behaviors?

Jana had just that experience. The wife of a successful dentist and the mother of two girls, aged 14 and 16, Jana was a school principal who was on the go all the time. She prided herself on being efficient and organized, and she managed to participate in community service as well as being actively involved with her children's lives, her marriage, and her job. She did everything to 100 percent of her capacity and was often recognized by others as successful. She had been an overachiever since she was a little girl. Her school trophies and awards were still on display in her house.

When she became a parent, Jana considered it her responsibility to make sure Felicia and Michelle were as successful as she was. Mom showed the girls her trophies and honors, thinking she was providing a good role model for them. But her belief that her success as a parent was tied to her children's success marked the beginning of the power struggles between them.

According to Felicia and Michelle, no matter what they did, they couldn't match their mom's achievements. As the girls entered high school, they became increasingly unmotivated. They began making excuses about missed assignments, and lying about participating in clubs and sports. They became lazy, their grades dropped, and they exploded in temperamental outbursts when challenged.

During therapy Jana was shocked to learn that both girls resented and feared having to compete with her high school record. She quickly realized that her focus on her children's achievements sacrificed a more spontaneous relationship. Jana's need for her daughters to succeed blinded her to who they really were. In effect, Felicia and Michelle had become her protégés instead of her daughters. They unconsciously resented this role and rebelled by their underachieving behaviors.

It is this tug of war between the unidentified subconscious needs of overachieving parents and underachieving children that renders the dynamic so "crazy-making" for both. On the surface, your goals seem totally positive and your child's response appears unreasonable. At deeper levels, however, an entirely different scenario is being acted out: Jana wanted her daughters to be just like her. She sought to mold them into her vision of success. She was unaware that her definition of success did not fit either daughter's preferences, choices, talents, or strengths.

Parenting with the hope of molding your child into an achiever isn't the issue. The difficulty occurs when your over-achieving attitudes prevent you from understanding who your child is. You may be highly motivated, competitive, perfectionistic, organized, energetic, and hard-working. You tend to define yourself in terms of the goals you achieve, goals that provide significant pragmatic rewards such as money, status, and public acknowledgment. Unfortunately, you may also expect your child to use the same criteria to define himself. However, children will not conform to your vision of who they are unless they agree with it. After all, they do have minds of their own.

Underachievement as an Escape from Responsibility

Like Jana, we often blur the boundaries between taking appropriate and inappropriate responsibility for our children's successes. It's hard to distinguish times when we are giving our children the discipline and support they need to achieve their own brand of success from the times that we deny them that achievement by making their successes our own. Often the clue is how pushy and overinvolved we become in work that is supposed to be theirs. You can help your children, guide them, and be a resource for them, but when you start dong their projects for them for fear they will fail, then you've overstepped your bounds. In short, if *you* take on responsibility for your kids' assignments, *they* don't have to be responsible for them.

Susan, looking extremely tired, came into my office with her 13-year-old son, David. She had been up half the night finishing David's science project while he slept comfortably. When I asked David to explain how he had managed to trick his mother into doing his work, he gave an embarrassed grin. "I was working on the project when my mom came home," he explained. "She told me that it looked sloppy. I had to finish it today, so I yelled at her to get off my back!"

Apparently that tactic didn't work. Susan explained that she stomped into the kitchen to start dinner and yelled back, "If you want to get a lousy grade, then fine!" But as she was making dinner she thought about how much David needed a good grade on this project in order to end up with a B in the class. During dinner she told David she would help him redo the sloppiest parts.

As the two worked, however, David's frustration grew; his mother griped continually about how he always put off assignments until the last minute. Finally David exploded. "I don't care if I get an F on this project," he yelled. "I'm going to bed."

"Come back and finish it," Susan shouted, but David did such a halfhearted job, she finally told him to go to bed.

Susan's overresponsibility for David's project allowed him to believe that procrastination was acceptable. He knew he didn't have to assume responsibility for himself because his mom would.

Typically, overachieving parents have high anxiety about failure of any kind. Indeed, you may need to rescue your child solely to relieve your own anxiety. Failing probably isn't an option you embrace easily, but unfortunately, failing is acceptable in your child's eyes. Chances are, you can't understand how anyone would choose to fail, while your child can't see why it's so important to succeed all the time. Because you want to believe that no one would ever choose to fail, you "help" your child inappropriately. Your unsolicited intervention actually reinforces underachieving behaviors.

If you recognize yourself in Susan, it wouldn't surprise me to learn that it's difficult for you to separate your personal success from your child's success and from your success as a parent. But it is critical that you draw a clear boundary between your responsibilities and those of your child. By staying on your side of the boundary consistently, you become a successful parent.

During therapy Susan defined to herself and then to her son what she was and was not willing to do. If David asked for help on further projects, he first had to list the tasks necessary to complete the assignment. Also he needed to make a tentative schedule to show how he was going to manage his time and his work. Then Susan would review David's plan and together they would decide what help he really needed. She would not participate in any of his projects if he didn't have a plan or if he waited until the last minute.

In the final analysis, we can't force our children to do anything. They are the ones who must define what success is for them and move toward it. We can only guide and support them in that journey. Of course, there are many ways of supporting a child's success that can be incorporated into parenting practices. These will unfold as we move through the material ahead.

Underachievement as a Response to Expectations

When working with overachieving parents, I always ask them to make two lists: one of what they expect from their children, and the other of what they expect from themselves. You may want to draw up these lists right now to help you become more aware of the attitudes shaping your parenting practices.

Being aware of expectations for yourself and your children is essential in order to recognize the messages you are giving them about who they should be. Too often, overachieving parents expect their children to:

- be able to set appropriate goals
- have the skills to complete them
- be self-disciplined enough to follow through
- delay gratification until they reach their goal
- be self-confident enough to overcome any self-doubt that might sabotage them
- know how to be organized
- use their time properly
- turn achievement into a sense of self-worth that will motivate them to take risks toward new goals

That's a tall order for anyone! As you read this list you can see how a child might easily be overwhelmed by these messages. When youngsters believe they can't meet such expectations, they develop underachieving behaviors to deal with their frustrations and sense of inadequacy.

I asked Bob and Lisa to draw up these lists when they came into my office complaining about their son Doug, age 10. Both recognized that Doug was an underachiever, but each had different opinions of what their son should be doing and how they should parent him. Bob and Lisa blamed each other for Doug's poor grades and laziness at home.

As these parents made a list of their expectations for themselves, Bob suddenly exclaimed, "Wow, the expectations I have for Doug are identical to the ones I have for myself!" Lisa realized the same about hers. When the couple compared lists and saw the difference in their expectations for themselves and hence for Doug, they finally understood why they were at odds on how to raise him.

Bob made being "Number One" a priority in everything he did. This is how he had lived his life, and since it worked for him, he thought it should work for his son. Bob was successful, had challenging goals, and enjoyed competition.

On the other hand, Lisa didn't see the point of competing.

She valued effort, feeling that if she tried her personal best that was achievement enough. Lisa had had difficulties in school because of a learning disability. Her teachers and parents encouraged her to avoid comparing her grades with others' because she was special. They reinforced effort, not grades.

The divergence in these personal attitudes led to different parenting approaches. Lisa helped Doug with his schoolwork whenever he asked because she thought he had tried to do it first by himself. Unfortunately, Doug was in the habit of automatically enlisting Lisa's help, partly because he realized his mom would jump in to rescue him and partly because he feared he couldn't achieve enough on his own to please his highly critical dad. Bob would make Doug redo assignments without showing him what was wrong or how to correct his mistakes. Predictably, this frustrated Doug and usually provoked him into a temper tantrum. Both parental behaviors—Lisa's help and Bob's criticism—were actually preventing the boy from learning the skills he needed in order to be independent.

Underachievers know exactly how their parents want them to behave. When I compare a child's list of what parents expect from him with the parents' list of expectations, they are virtually identical. But although the child may be aware of parental expectations, they don't automatically become the child's code of behavior. As your expectations become the criteria for judging your child, you undermine your child's sense of self.

Bob was angry at Lisa because he felt she was babying Doug; Lisa was angry with Bob because she felt he criticized Doug too harshly instead of helping him. During therapy, both parents recognized that they couldn't transfer their personal expectations to Doug. It was important for them to recognize their son's unique strengths and weaknesses and then to develop parenting practices to work with these.

As they did so, it became clear that Doug could usually complete his homework satisfactorily on his own. The grades he earned were mostly C's and B's, but he felt happy with these because they were his. Now that he didn't have all his emotions tied up with the daily homework problem, he had the time and energy to learn how to raise and care for Guide Dog puppies. Eventually, he became quite an expert at this, and his new success transferred over to his grades. Before long Doug was on the honor roll at school. By this point, Bob had realized that his son's goals and interests were different from his own, and Lisa had realized that she didn't need to rescue Doug from his homework or his father's criticism.

Underachievement as a Cry for Help

Whenever I work with underachieving children, I ask them if they want to get good grades. Without exception each child responds positively. Children have a natural desire to learn and achieve. But often youngsters feel they don't know how to accomplish their goals and may be too embarrassed to ask for help. Many underachieving behaviors are a response to these frustrations. In such cases, underachievement is really an unspoken cry for help. Underachievers need emotional support and specific skills to make them successful. But as a parent you may feel helpless if your child needs assistance and you don't know what to say or do.

Sally, age 12, was telling her mom, Tracy, that she was completing her math assignments when in reality she wasn't. Her lies finally caught up with her when she got an F on her report card. Both her parents were furious because Sally hadn't asked them for help in two months. When they confronted her and demanded to know why, she began to cry and wouldn't speak.

When I asked Sally what it was like for her to ask for help, she said she felt "stupid." "The way my mom explains it to me doesn't help because she does it differently than my teacher. This just confuses me more. And if I ask questions, my mom gets impatient and says, 'I don't see why you don't understand!' Then my mom just repeats the explanation using the same words."

Sally needed Tracy to be more flexible in her explanations. But Tracy felt a helplessness bordering on failure because she saw she wasn't getting through to her daughter. Her solution was to put the burden back on Sally, telling her that she needed to pay attention when someone was explaining things to her. Tracy's reprimands were so demoralizing for Sally that she found it easier to lie and fail on her own than to feel stupid and responsible for her mother's failure as a tutor.

During a therapy session, Tracy finally saw that the methods she was using to teach math were not wrong but dated. She released her feelings of being inadequate in helping her daughter. After looking over Sally's math book, she quickly understood the new math and was now able to help Sally.

Underachievement as a Cry for Attention

Children want and need attention. They will try to get it in many ways until they find one that works for them. Attention can come in the form of recognizing accomplishments or spending time together. As a busy parent your time is limited, and if your child hasn't accomplished something noteworthy by your standards, he may not get enough attention from you. Since attention validates that he exists, your child will get your attention in one way or another—sometimes in a negative way.

Twelve-year-old Derek hated it when his mother nagged him to do his homework every day, but at least her nagging made him feel that she cared about him. It was proof she knew he existed. From Derek's point of view, his older sister, Bonnie, got all the attention in the house. Bonnie was an honor student and director of the school play. Derek saw how excited and attentive his parents were when Bonnie talked about her accomplishments. He also knew how much his mother bragged about Bonnie to her friends. Derek didn't want to hate his sister, but he was so jealous of the attention she got that he often irritated her, which caused more problems with his parents. Seeing Bonnie be acknowledged for her achievements made Derek feel isolated from his family. The only time his parents talked to him was when he misbehaved or relinquished responsibility for himself. So naturally, he acted out all the more.

As Derek had discovered, negative attention is better than no attention at all. Of course, negative interactions only reinforce the child's feelings of inadequacy and continue to activate the parent's anger. Parent and child are caught in a reactive cycle that supports the underachieving behaviors. Only when an underachieving child and his parents learn new communication skills can this cycle be broken. (See chapter 7.) Indeed, when Derek's parents applied the communication skills they learned at a parenting workshop, they were able to listen attentively to their son. This gave Derek the positive attention he needed and was the beginning of an improved family life.

Underachievement as a Way to Wrest Control from an Authoritarian Parent

Successful people take charge in order to get things done. In your job you are probably considered an authority, with defined tasks and expectations for yourself and for how others will treat you. Your job gives you power to carry out your responsibilities. But as a parent, there are no guidelines on how to use power and authority appropriately—no job description. Often, lacking a clear definition of parental power, parents equate authority with their desire to get their child to do what they want. But as you have already seen, forcing your child to toe the line at any cost may be wrong for him.

Thirteen-year-old Tom refused to do any homework or participate in family activities. Although he had exhibited rebellious behavior since he was a small boy, he became unmanageable as he grew into adolescence. He was defiant, defensive, and belligerent. Most recently, the school principal accused him of stealing money from the student store.

When Tom's parents, Ray and Beth, came into my office, they were fearful that their son's antisocial behavior would escalate. Ray was a successful salesperson whose presence overshadowed that of his wife and son. He had strong ideas about how Tom should behave and he was disgusted with his son's rebellion, which he was determined to stop. "Since Tom was a little boy," Ray said, "I always had to be tough with him to make him do things right." That meant giving Tom orders. Ray expected to be obeyed without question. If Tom dared to defy him, Ray punished him severely.

In response, Tom said, "My dad is always telling me what to do without ever listening to what I have to say. Anything I do isn't good enough for him. I'm tired of people controlling my life." Recently, Tom threatened to run away if his father hit him or sent him to his room again. As he put it, "I just want everyone off my back!"

Tom felt he had no control over his own life. The only time he felt he had any power was when he refused his father's demands. But this vengeful false control actually prevented Tom from participating in the experiences that could have supported a sense of real control. In Ray's attempt to force his son to be successful, he had been controlling, domineering, and unresponsive to the boy's true needs. Tom mastered underachieving behaviors as a way of preserving a sense of self.

As I worked with the family to open up the lines of communication, Tom realized that revenge was too high a price to pay to feel in control. He began to take part in decisions affecting his life. During this new openness in relating, Tom became willing to learn the skills necessary to be responsible for himself. And Ray, in turn, realized that his son was a person of value in his own right.

Underachievement as a Way to Cope with Disapproval

Underachieving children sabotage themselves when they know they are not acting the way their parents want them to. Parents use their authority to inform their children in a variety of ways that they are displeased with their behavior. In an overachieving family, it is quite clear that the way to get love and acceptance is to excel. It doesn't take long for an underachieving child in such a family to recognize that she is out of sync. Because children learn from their parents how to view themselves, it should come as no surprise that underachieving children label themselves negatively just as their parents do. Each time a parent criticizes, puts down, yells at, or punishes a child, her bad feelings about herself are confirmed.

Children reinforce these defeatist attitudes through negative self-talk. I have heard underachieving youngsters say, "I just can't do anything right," "Nothing I do is good enough," "I'm a failure," and "Oh God, I'm so stupid. I hate myself." These are spoken versions of silent statements they make to themselves all day.

Such negative self-talk and the underachieving that goes with it are symptoms of the alienation some children feel because they believe it's impossible to be like their mother or father. Often parents erroneously interpret these behaviors as permanent personality traits. They don't realize that behaviors differ from personality traits. Behaviors are a result of thinking and feeling, while personality traits are inherent in the individual. Chapter 3 will help you distinguish behaviors that are true expressions of your child's personality from those that are responses to your actions.

In an attempt to handle the pain and pressure they feel, underachieving children are experts at devising ways to escape reality. Whether it be daydreaming in the classroom, exaggerating stories about themselves with their friends, or becoming TV or computer addicts, underachieving children will do whatever it takes to get their minds off their feelings of inadequacy. Because they need to escape a situation they feel powerless to change, they are at high risk for drug or alcohol abuse and other self-destructive behaviors. Many teenage clients I've worked with who were involved with drugs were also underachievers from an early age.

For example, Barbara, age 16, got involved with a group of kids who used illegal drugs because she believed they accepted her for who she was. At first Barbara felt frightened of drugs, but as she used them more and more, she found them a convenient escape from the pressures her parents put on her. "When I'm high I don't have to worry about anything!" she told me. "I don't care about what's happening to me because my parents really didn't care either. All they worry about is if I get the same grades as my sister. They love her, not me."

In her self-destructive way, Barbara was crying out for acceptance and love from her parents. She wanted and needed to be told that she was a person of worth.

In actuality, Barbara's parents were desperately worried about her. They were confused and anxious about their parenting skills. Unaware of Barbara's perception, they thought they had treated the two girls equally. Unconsciously, they were expecting identical behavior in response, yet one daughter was succeeding whereas the other was in serious trouble. They felt bewildered, vaguely guilty, and angry at Barbara for what they perceived as her deliberate and unreasonable rejection. They had yet to understand that it was Barbara who felt unappreciated and rejected. Once they did, they were able to express their true feelings and thoughts to their daughter. This opened the way to solving their problems.

Behind the underachieving behaviors of children are messages of need:

- David procrastinated on his science project because he didn't know how to organize it.
- Doug felt unsupported by his father because he couldn't meet his dad's expectations.
- Sally needed to be reassured that it was okay to not understand something.
- Derek needed attention.
- Tom needed his father's acceptance.
- Barbara needed to be loved.

Whether your child is crying for help, wants attention, or is battling for control, her underachieving behavior is her way to get you to stop and listen.

Chapter Three

Do You Recognize Your Child?

Temperament Styles • Different Ways of Thinking • Learning Disabilities

T he natural differences between you and your child can affect your perception of her. These differences, if unrecognized or misunderstood, often result in arguments, hurt feelings, and alienation. As a parent, you may erroneously see your child's behaviors and actions as resistance, disrespect, or defiance when in fact they are evidence of differing temperament or thinking styles, or perhaps even learning disabilities. Let's explore these issues more carefully so that you better understand your child.

Temperament Styles

You and your child share the same home environment and many experiences. But each of you has a natural temperament that predisposes you to your own way of learning, relating to others and self, being motivated, and feeling satisfied. Since your temperament style may differ from your youngster's, she may judge and perceive the same stimulus differently than you.

The great Swiss physician-psychologist Carl Jung developed the concept of temperaments to explain human personality. He observed that human behavior fell into patterns of particular personality traits rather than being a series of random occurrences. One way to classify these patterns is by temperament style. Your temperament describes your totality, whereas a personality trait is only one aspect of you. Consequently, it is unproductive—even damaging—to ask your child to change her temperament style. In effect, you are asking her to be someone else. When you attempt to change your child's temperament, you are trying to take away part of her innate personality and deny her selfhood. Rebellion under these circumstances is natural.

Your child may share some traits with you, but since these are influenced by the whole person, the traits may be expressed differently. That's what happened in my family. Even though my husband, John, and my stepdaughter Julie are competitive, intelligent, and hard working, their approaches to accomplishing tasks are very different. John's temperament is characterized by a structured style of working: He creates a list of tasks and deadlines and then carefully adheres to it. Julie's is spontaneous: She works whenever it suits her mood. Before John understood temperament styles, he and his daughter fought frequently. John criticized Julie's approach as irresponsible. He tried to make her behave his way. John perceived as underachieving behaviors Julie's natural disposition to work spontaneously. Of course, his demands were met with rebellion because Julie couldn't change her temperament style, even to please her father.

When you understand temperament factors, you can easily recognize your child's style. Temperament styles are neither good nor bad, but we may respond negatively to those that are different from our own. What follows is a model of temperament factors based on Jung's theory. This information will equip you to help your child—using her unique style.

Introverted/Extroverted

Introverts relate more easily to the inner world of ideas than to the outer world of people and things. They enjoy private places in their minds and environments, and charge their batteries by engaging in solitary activities, working alone, reading, meditating, playing individual sports, and participating in activities that include only a few people.

Extroverts, on the other hand, relate more easily to the outer world of people and things than to the inner world of ideas. These are the individuals who need to be around others to charge their batteries. Because they spend a good deal of time in the company of people, they are more likely than introverts to have sophisticated socialization skills.

An extroverted child always wants to play with his friends. He becomes lonely when he is by himself. An introverted child can be lonely within a group of children and often chooses to play by himself or read. According to Isabel Briggs Myers, who developed the Myers-Briggs Type Indicator, a test based on Jung's theory, 75 percent of Western population are extroverts. Western culture seems to sanction the outgoing, sociable, and gregarious temperament (in contrast to many Eastern cultures).

Since extroversion is so predominant in our society, introversion often becomes suspect. Extroverts regard aloneness as what one does until something better comes along—namely—being with others. Classmates of the introverted child can misunderstand his natural desire to be alone or with few people (and can make fun of him), leading to his feeling alienated. Similar clashes of temperament can occur between parent and child. The need for differing quantities of "alone" and "together time" can be misconstrued between parent and child as a lack of caring for one another.

When my stepdaughter Jill and I first started living together, I experienced the misunderstandings that can occur between introverts and extroverts. Jill is an extrovert and I am an introvert. I needed time alone after seeing clients or conducting workshops in order to recharge and be in harmony with myself. Jill, on the other hand, is happiest when she is talking with others. As my husband says, "Jill's conversation is one continuous sentence devoid of periods or commas." When we first began living together, Jill interpreted my need for alone time as a rejection of her. She felt hurt because I couldn't give her the attention she needed. I, on the other hand, thought her demands were overwhelming and inconsiderate.

As a consequence of the dissonance in our temperaments, Jill felt alienated from me. In protest of my not meeting her needs, she stopped following the homework schedule that we had set up. After the third time that I tiptoed into my bedroom after work (so she wouldn't hear me come in), I knew I had to look at the situation.

Because we hadn't addressed the differences in our temperament styles, our interactions had been strained and difficult. But when Jill and I talked over our introversion and extroversion, we immediately felt closer. "You always looked so annoyed whenever I talked to you. I felt I was bothering you," Jill explained. "Then when you started to avoid me I thought you didn't like me."

I told her, "Being alone is my way of staying centered and relaxed. I enjoy hearing your stories and talking with you but it never seemed enough for you." We came up with a plan to deal with our disparate needs: I would say "Hi" to Jill when I came in the door and go to my room for a half an hour of quiet time. After my break, I would be ready and able to enjoy her company.

For her part, Jill admitted that she engaged in "recreational talking"—talking just for the fun of it—in addition to communicating because she needed to share information or ask for my input. We decided that when I started feeling overwhelmed with recreational talking I would say, "Jill, I'm on overload." At that point she would simply call one of her friends to meet her conversational needs. The plan worked well! We enjoyed each other while respecting our individual styles of relating.

Jill's extroverted temperament also created conflicts around her use of time. I judged her need to be with others as wasting time. I felt she could better use those hours on her schoolwork. But doing homework is a solitary activity that was predictably torturous for her. That explained our problems with getting her to complete assignments. We needed to develop a way to use Jill's natural social ability to support her to do her homework. She started bringing two of her girlfriends home to do schoolwork together. Since I had a personal bias against this approach, I intently watched how the girls worked. To my surprise, they stayed on task, completed their work, helped each other study, improved their grades, and had fun in the process!

Extroverted parents who have an introverted child often think that their child's need for alone time is a result of a personal problem. They may believe that something must be wrong with their child if he chooses to read in his room instead of playing with friends. As a result, the extroverted parent puts more pressure on the child to participate in activities. Frequently, the demands of an extroverted parent can be unreasonable for an introverted child.

Sonnie was an extrovert who feared that life was going to pass by her 12-year-old, Nancy. She couldn't understand what caused her daughter to be a loner. She wanted Nancy to be more sociable and outgoing with girls her own age. To accomplish this, Sonnie became a Girl Scout leader and insisted that Nancy join the group. Unfortunately, each time Sonnie told Nancy to speak up or talk more to the other girls in the troop, Nancy withdrew. During therapy Nancy explained, "I don't know why I don't care about being with friends all the time. But there must be something wrong with me because my mom gets so upset when I spend time alone in my room. I hate it when she tells me to be more sociable. I only want to talk when I feel like it."

Sonnie thought being an extrovert was necessary to be successful in life. She feared that her daughter's quiet ways would be interpreted by others as self-doubt.

As I described the traits of extroversion and introversion, both mother and daughter were able to look at their differences nonjudgmentally. Sonnie felt relieved that Nancy was not a misfit. Nancy realized that her desire to be alone was a normal reaction to being around too many people for too long. Without Sonnie pressuring Nancy to join in more with others, the girl was able to develop her own rhythm of appropriate social and alone time. As a result she felt more at ease when interacting with others.

Recognizing the introvert/extrovert dynamics in your family will help you make decisions that support your child's need for interactive and alone time.

Thinking/Feeling

A thinking person bases decisions on impersonal data and logic. A feeling person bases decisions on personal reactions and experience. Nevertheless, thinking types do have feelings, and feelers are able to think! It is just a matter of preference or comfort.

Thinking types may not show intense emotions even though they may experience them. Feeling types show their emotions intensely. Depending on one's preference, either style can be viewed positively or negatively. Thus, thinking types can be labeled cold, impersonal, and hard or logical, objective, and level-headed. Feelers can be perceived as scatterbrained, unstable, and illogical or warm, caring, and human.

The relationship that feeling children have with authority figures can influence their ability to achieve. For example, if a feeling child really likes his teacher he is more apt to work hard in class. If he feels the teacher, coach, or parent doesn't like him he will give up trying or refuse to complete the task at hand. Feeling children experience hurt and rejection when they believe they are not liked. They consequently withdraw from or become uncooperative with those who hurt them.

Thinking children need a logical reason to cooperate with authority figures. Before they can learn from a teacher, they need to respect the instructor and believe that he or she is competent in the subject matter. Furthermore, they tend to achieve in subjects that mentally stimulate them, often at the expense of those that don't. That's why they are inconsistent or perform inadequately in certain subjects, even though they have the ability to do well. At times, they can appear to be miniature adults.

My relationship with Jill provides another example of different temperament styles. I am a thinking type and Jill is a feeling type. True to form, I believed that once we objectively defined Jill's goals for grades, wrote down what she needed to do, and structured her time in a logical manner, she would be able to improve her performance. But Jill proved me wrong. Even with the logical plan, she continued to do poorly. When she resisted my logical reasons to get good grades, I became angrier and angrier with her.

Finally, by recognizing Jill as a feeling person, I realized she needed to find a reason why getting good grades was important to *her*. That's when we came up with the concept of tying grades to her use of the car. If she maintained a B average with no grade lower than a C, she could drive. With anything lower she was not allowed to drive until she had written proof from her teachers that she had regained a B average. That certainly provided the immediate persuasion. But Jill also had to figure out a subjective meaning to getting good grades. We hit pay dirt when Jill recognized that she loved to play volleyball and wanted to play at the college level. This provided her with the personal impetus to pursue grades high enough to qualify for acceptance at a college that had a good volleyball program.

If I hadn't recognized Jill's feeling temperament, I would have continued to be angry, disappointed, and critical with her. Most likely, this would have caused her to suffer a diminished sense of self. She might even have become rebellious.

When working with underachieving children, you need to help the thinking youngster logically determine the importance of achieving; you need to help the feeling child find a reason why achievement is personally important to him.

Organized/Spontaneous

Most achievers identify with organized persons, those who have a strong work ethic and put business before pleasure. Organized people establish and take deadlines seriously and expect others to do the same. They provide stability and maintain organizations so that they function smoothly and efficiently. They are loyal, sensible, dependable, practical, and responsible.

Spontaneous people use a deadline not as a goal for finishing work, but as a signal to start. Rather than a work ethic, they have a "play ethic" that allows them to fool around before their tasks are done. Freedom is important to them because it allows them to act on their impulses. They like activities in which they are independent and enjoy freedom of movement. Spontaneous types are bold, lighthearted, thrill-seeking, action-orientated, competitive, and impulsive.

Organized people often describe spontaneous people as indecisive, procrastinating, immature, and unrealistic. Spontaneous types describe organizers as rigid, inflexible, driven, and too task-oriented.

If you have an organized child, you are probably pleased with his academic progress. Organized children have a strong sense of right and wrong and enjoy following the rules and regulations of school. They respect authority and feel safe and comfortable in the structure of the school system. For spontaneous children, however, school is extremely difficult. They need physical and experiential involvement in the learning process. Lectures, reading, or routine drill work are unappealing to them. Natural competitiveness and a sense of fun are their motivators to participate in school.

Danielle came into my office depressed and discouraged. An organized person, she was mother to Peter, a nine-year-old spontaneous child. "I have tried everything to get him to pay attention to me when I help him with his homework. We end up fighting every night. I just can't do this anymore," cried Danielle. Danielle had been trying to help Peter memorize the multiplication tables by drilling him. The monotony of the drill along with her repeated instructions to sit still were at odds with the boy's temperament.

When Danielle recognized the differences between her temperament type and her son's, she was relieved to know why their relationship had become so difficult. We devised a method in which Peter could demonstrate to his mother his knowledge of multiplication facts by using blocks. Red blocks represented the ones, blue blocks the tens. Peter could make any design he wanted with the blocks as long as they represented the answer. Then he also gave his mother the answer verbally.

Although this method took more time than the rote drill at first, by getting physically involved with the process Peter learned his times tables quickly. The tension between mother and son disappeared, and a new cooperative attitude prevailed.

Sensing/Intuitive

A sensing person perceives with his five senses. He has the ability to see the world as it is, since he makes decisions based on observable and practical facts. He focuses attention on what others say and do. Sensers trust conventional and customary behavior and try new approaches only in relation to past experiences that have already proved workable.

The intuitive person perceives with memory and association, patterns and meaning, and possibilities. He has the ability to read between the lines, to see the big picture, and to rely on hunches. He trusts his inspiration rather than past experience, and prefers to use new approaches to solve problems or make decisions. His developed intuition provides insight into complex thought; an ability to see abstract, symbolic, and theoretical relationships; and a capacity to see future possibilities creatively.

When I was teaching algebra to eighth-grade students, I readily recognized the differences between these two temperament styles. After explaining a new concept, I would model it by doing a few problems on the board. I showed a step-by-step progression to work out the problem. When it came time for the class to practice a problem I'd written on the board, the sensing students would follow each step methodically. The intuitive, in contrast, would work it out using an abstract process. Indeed, they would frequently blurt out the answer before most others had finished. When I asked the intuitive students to explain how they had arrived at the answer so quickly, they would come up with a creative use of theoretical relationships. Since I am an intuitive type, I found it great fun to follow their thinking. However, it was difficult to convince the intuitive students to use a step-by-step *procedure*, which was necessary for more advanced concepts.

It is more likely that sensing parents will misunderstand the intuitive child than vice versa. Intuitive youngsters dream up creative ideas and excellent solutions but may be unable to substantiate how they arrived at their conclusions or to bring their ideas into reality.

The way a teacher structures assignments such as reports or projects may meet with resistance from intuitive children. They see a step-by-step approach as a waste of time. Indeed, they understand how to do a task, but they may approach it in a unique manner so that the teacher may question whether it was done correctly.

Moreover, it is difficult for intuitive youngsters to do routine work, especially if it has many details. For this reason they may not finish their homework even though they understand the assignment. Their failure to complete assignments can easily frustrate parents. Furthermore, they tend to anticipate what a parent or teacher is about to say instead of actually listening. This might make it seem they are deliberately ignoring instructions. Asking the intuitive child to repeat instructions helps him focus on the specific requests.

You can learn a great deal about your child through this concept of temperament styles. If you want more information on them, *Please Understand Me: An Essay on Temperament Styles,* by David Keirsey and Marilyn Bates, can be most helpful (see Bibliography).

Different Ways of Thinking

Like temperament styles, each person has a unique way of thinking. Here again it is important to be aware of how your child's style may differ from yours. This will prevent you from misjudging or misunderstanding natural diversity. Although there are many psychological models to describe the various ways people think, I've chosen two that are most relevant to understanding the differences that can exist between over- and underachieving.

Conceptual/Specific

A *conceptual* thinker is one who is most comfortable dealing with ideas. He needs to see the whole picture first in order to understand where all the component pieces fit. This gives him a way to understand the interrelationship of ideas. The *specific* thinker is one who builds the whole picture by taking one piece at a time and fitting it together with others.

If a conceptual and a specific thinker were sitting side by side, each working on his own jigsaw puzzle, you would clearly see how differently they organize reality. The conceptual thinker would pick one idea or concept to work on, such as the sky or ground, until the puzzle was completed. The specific thinker, on the other hand, would gather pieces that fit together. He might look for all the straight edged pieces first and then assemble all the pieces of like color. Eventually, the different images would appear to make the whole.

If your child is one type of thinker and you are another, you may have thought that she wasn't paying attention when you were talking or she wasn't trying when you helped her with her homework. Conceptual children want to know *why* and specific thinkers want to know *how*. If both types are in eighth grade studying War World II, the conceptual thinker will want to know why the war started before she is willing to study the dates, battles, and consequences. The specific thinker will want to know how and when it happened. She'll focus on the specifics one battle at a time.

Once you've identified which type of thinker your child is, you can keep in mind the approach she needs when you give instructions, share ideas, or help with homework.

Right-Brain/Left-Brain Dominance

Researchers continue to explore the complexities of the brain. Today it is accepted that the brain has two sides (hemispheres) that are linked. While each person uses both sides of the brain, each individual tends to use one or the other side predominantly.

The left side of the brain deals with logic, language, reasoning, numbers, and linear, sequential thinking. The right side deals with rhythm, music, images and imagination, color, daydreaming, and the creative processes.

Most school activities such as learning to read, reason, and compute in a logical and sequential manner are based on left-brain functions. Therefore, if your child is a left-brain-dominant child she may have an easier time at school. She will more readily respond to analysis and a logical approach to finding solutions than a right-side-dominant child will.

To support your right-side-brain child, it is still important to use logic and structure but you should also allow her to use her strengths. For example, a right-brain child may memorize facts more readily if she can creatively put them into a song she has made up. She may remember her spelling words better if she draws pictures next to them that relate to the words. Whenever possible, support her in using her imagination to help her understand and learn concepts and facts. Have her make up a story about something she has learned in social studies or science so that she can use her imagination.

To work with a right-side-dominant child you need to help her express what she knows creatively. This often means finding a way that is different from many of her schoolmates' learning methods or her teacher's suggestions. If you actively support and appreciate your youngster's creativity, she will accept it as the gift it is and not judge her unique way as something that separates her from others.

Learning Disabilities

While it is not the aim of this book to present a definitive study in learning disabilities, it is important for parents to be aware of them. Parents may observe underachieving behaviors and fail to recognize that a learning disability may have contributed to the problem.

In the broadest sense of the word, learning disabilities refer to learning difficulties that are associated with factors such as mental retardation, brain injury, impaired vision, hearing difficulties, and emotional disturbances. In its narrow sense, the term refers to a child who fails to acquire academic skills even though he has adequate intelligence, maturation, and cultural background.

Reading problems are the most common learning disability. Reading requires the transformation of visual symbols into verbal language. The reading-disabled child may see letters or words reversed or may not comprehend what he has read.

Attention-deficit disorder is another disability that can appear as rebellious behavior but is in fact a brain dysfunction. Children with this disability have difficulty paying attention in class and staying on task. These children struggle to organize and complete their work. They may require twice as much time as their peers to complete assignments because their attention wanders.

Many normal behaviors, however, can be similar to the behaviors of learning-disabled children. By keeping in touch with your child's teacher and getting feedback about her progress, you can better recognize whether a potential problem exists. You may be able to make a determination by observing the learning process. If you or your child's teacher recognizes that Jessica can understand and assimilate information but chooses not to do her work, then most likely she's exhibiting underachieving behaviors. But if Jessica has difficulty reading or understanding material she *wants* to read for her own interests, then it would be advisable to investigate learning disabilities.

Pam came to my office convinced that her child had an attention-deficit problem with hyperactivity. (Children with attention-deficit disorders are divided in two types: those who exhibit hyperactivity with the disorder and those who do not.) She felt such a diagnosis would be a relief for her, because at least then she could identify the problem.

"How long does Mark sit in front of the TV?" I asked. "Oh, hours," Pam replied. "When is it difficult for Mark to pay attention?" I asked.

"Mostly when I help him with his homework and in school."

"If Mark had an attention-deficit disorder with hyperactivity," I explained, "he couldn't be able to sit and watch TV for hours."

When observing your child for possible learning disabilities, it's important to take into account his motivation level. There is a big difference between "I can't" and "I won't."

Schools are able to test children for learning disabilities, and there are special programs for the learning-disabled. In working with learning-disabled children, I have been able to help them by using the same techniques and strategies I advocate in this book. I would suggest first using these techniques to improve your child's skills, for these are the same skills he will need if he does have a learning disability.

Distinguishing the natural differences between you and your child will help you better identify his underachieving behaviors. In the next chapter you will see that underachieving behaviors also have patterns. With the information from this chapter and the next, you will be able to discriminate between temperament styles, different ways of thinking, learning disabilities, and underachieving behaviors.

Chapter Four

Different Children, Different Patterns of Behavior

Types of Underachievers

In my years of working with parents and children, I have identified five types of underachievers, based on behavior. These types include the:

- people-pleaser

- procrastinator

- excuse-maker

- master manipulator

- dropout

When you can zero in on your child's behavior patterns, you'll be better equipped to support her in moving from a self-defeating attitude to positive self-esteem. Not only will you help her change her behavior, you'll also assist her in altering self-sabotaging thinking patterns and master self-defeating feelings.

You may recognize aspects of your child in more than one of the following descriptions. If you do, observe what triggers a particular response. Your youngster may adapt to certain situations or specific people. For instance, you may discover she is a master manipulator with you and a people-pleaser with her teacher. At various times, you have to deal with the dynamics of both types of underachievement.

Let's look at the five underachievement styles more closely. Bear in mind that we'll examine both the thinking patterns and the underlying feelings common to each behavior.

The People-Pleaser

Behaviors:	Appeases, cooperates, works hard, acts sensitive and frightened
Thinking Style:	*Internal messages:* "If I make my parents happy they will love me." "If I do something wrong my parents will be angry with me." *External messages:* "Am I doing this right?" "What do you want me to do?"
Feelings:	Insecurity, anxiety, fear of rejection and abandonment

As their name implies, people-pleasers are so busy making sure they are doing what parents, coaches, teachers, and other authority figures want, they never risk an activity that may have meaning just for them.

As soon as the people-pleaser garners approval in any direction, her standards are set. Rarely does she set goals higher than or different from what the authority figures expect. Consequently, she seldom ventures beyond a safe, secure position. Unfortunately, the persistent desire for safety can be a limitation since only through trial and error will a child recognize and understand her unique strengths and talents.

The need for continuous approval tends to make a people-pleaser dependent on parents, teachers, and other adults as she accomplishes schoolwork, chores, or other activities. Her growth toward true independence, therefore, can be inhibited.

Jackie, age nine, wanted to please her parents and teacher and tried to do everything to meet their standards. Her teacher, Mrs. Rogers, asked the students to write a paragraph about a butterfly, using three sentences under the topic sentence. Jackie had many more ideas for her paragraph, but she didn't write them because she feared it would upset Mrs. Rogers. When the teacher read Jackie's paper to the class as an example of a good paragraph, Jackie felt relieved that she hadn't put her additional thoughts into the assignment. This pattern of pleasing people became so ingrained that Jackie would spend hours on an assignment to make sure she got it just right. "Right" to Jackie meant figuring out what would win approval from Mrs. Rogers.

Although this was not the teacher's intent, such selective approval discouraged Jackie from exploring her own creative expression. Her need for approval made her stay within the narrow scope of the requirements and overshadowed her willingness to risk using her real abilities. Jackie feared that to go beyond the scope of her teacher's expectations would bring disapproval. Because she had to mask her true creative nature, this child began getting stomach aches in school.

During therapy sessions, Jackie and her parents recognized that the stomach aches were caused by anxiety. If Jackie was told she was doing well, she felt safe and secure; but if the teacher didn't provide constant positive feedback, she feared she was making Mrs. Rogers angry. Jackie equated showing her true abilities with receiving disapproval. The fear of abandonment looms large in a child's subconscious when she feels accepted only if she does exactly what others require.

Youngsters draw this conclusion when parents consciously or subconsciously give love as a sign of approval and withdraw it to show disapproval. This emotional seesaw causes children to become insecure, thus producing appeasing behavior. As you will see in chapter 8, it is important for children to learn to take appropriate risks based on their own choices and decisions. Helping a child to reframe failure as an opportunity to learn will strengthen her self-image.

People-pleasers may be difficult to identify as underachievers because they are cooperative at home and make a teacher's life easy. Indeed, instructors can and do misread these youngsters' desire to please as a true need to learn. What distinguishes people-pleasers from achieving students is their fear of mistakes. Since they don't risk expressing original opinions or thoughts, they are not truly developing their own abilities but merely reflecting what they perceive parents, teachers, and other adults require. Being externally motivated, their sense of self is underdeveloped. People-pleasers often fail to recognize who they are because they are busy reading other people's reactions. Within many people-pleasers are hidden writers, artists, oceanographers, doctors. But these youngsters are afraid of pursuing their own dreams because they haven't developed the emotional strength to follow their own path. They allow others to determine their paths for them.

When people-pleasers fail, not only must they deal with the pressure of failure, but they also feel guilty about failing. To their way of thinking, they should always be successful. If they are not, they feel they did something wrong and let down the most important people in their lives. They also violated their own prime directive for survival. This kind of thinking translates into negative self-talk such as:

- "I'm bad."

- "There's something wrong with me."

- "I don't deserve love."

- "I can't do anything right."

- "Now Mom will hate me."

Eric, a second-grader, was a hard worker at school and was only happy and secure when his teacher commented on his successes. At home, he put his toys away after play, made his bed in the morning, and dressed and undressed himself. One morning his mother, Julie, commented, "Eric, you are such a good boy!" as she saw him cleaning up his toys. She was shocked when he came over and kicked her. Julie thought this was an isolated incident and she forgot about it. But the following week Eric had a similar outburst, and Julie became concerned.

She called Eric's school and asked about his classroom behavior. Eric's teacher cited several recent instances in which the youngster misbehaved a few minutes after she had complimented him in front of the class. Eric's outbursts continued to escalate, and finally Julie brought him to therapy.

In session, we discovered that Eric had grown used to doing well in school and getting the approval he needed, but as the class started learning subtraction, he found it difficult to keep up. Because he was making some mistakes—an unusual turn of events for him—he felt as if he were a failure. He thought himself unworthy of praise. As Eric said in a session, "I'm a bad boy." Because of this negative attitude, he couldn't accept the positive comments from his mother or teacher; he had to prove them wrong by misbehaving.

As Eric understood his relationship to authority figures, he was supposed to please them in order to be worthy to receive their love and acceptance. This dependency on acting according to someone else's standards in order to receive nurturing makes it impossible for people-pleasers to define themselves. They are too entangled in the reactions of others to see themselves as separate and unique.

In therapy, Eric's parents learned to ask him how he thought and felt about everyday situations. They constructed family situations to allow him to learn the consequences of his choices. This helped him recognize that his behavior was a reflection of his own sense of self and that he could be loved and accepted by authority figures even if he made mistakes from time to time.

The Procrastinator

Behavior:	Procrastinates, rationalizes
Thinking Style:	*Internal Messages:* "I can't do this." "Where on earth do I start?" *External Messages:* "I'll do it later." "It's not important—I'll hurry through it." "I'll do it tomorrow."
Feelings:	Inadequacy, insecurity, frustration, anger, confusion, guilt

Procrastinators put off their schoolwork and chores until the last minute and then do the job with the intent of just getting it over with. They never engage all of their skills and abilities in the task.

Procrastination is an expression of our children's fear that they will be less competent than we expect. Procrastinators won't risk working as hard as they can, for fear of finding out they can't reach the standards we set for them. It's easier to have reasons why one doesn't do well than to actually discover one's limitations.

When Johnny got an F on his math test, he rationalized, "Well, I didn't study for it anyway, so big deal." The fear of failure was so threatening to him that he couldn't risk studying and failing. By never finding out their true abilities, procrastinators believe they won't have to experience parental disappointment or their own. Nevertheless, this cover-up doesn't alleviate their sense of inadequacy.

When procrastinators consider a task, they experience tension at the mere thought of doing it. Consequently, procrastinators often engage in "busy work" instead of their assignments to help relieve the tension.

Keri came home from school and was supposed to do her homework immediately, but first she had to eat. The snack became a major event that used up an hour of her time. Then she thought she would give a girlfriend a call, which turned into an hour-and-a-half talkathon. When she realized her mother would be home soon, she dashed off to her room and hurried through her homework. Habitually, Keri focused neither attention nor creative effort on her work.

Eating and talking on the phone helped Keri escape the tension she felt about facing her assignments. Other escape techniques include watching TV, reading, going out with friends, daydreaming, cleaning out drawers or tidying up a room, and drawing.

Sometimes procrastinators' diversions are designed to stop their parents from criticizing them. For example, when Kathy's mother, Ruth, banished her to her room one Sunday morning to finish a book report due the following day, she was astonished to find Kathy's room spotless when she checked two hours later. Ruth didn't know how to react. "I'm delighted to see the room cleaned," she finally said, "but I'm angry the book report still hasn't been touched."

Kathy replied, "I just can't work in such a mess!" To Kathy, cleaning the room was a worthwhile activity. Besides, she derived a sense of satisfaction from it that she knew she wouldn't get from agonizing over her book report. Other procrastinators make lists of lists, organize the materials involved in an assignment, or clean out notebooks and backpacks to rationalize their avoidance of a dreaded task.

Procrastinators also distract their parents or teachers, causing them to forget the issue at hand. Kevin, age 11, was supposed to rake up the leaves and mow the lawn right after breakfast on Saturday mornings. One Saturday he took an unusually long time at breakfast, playing with his food. While his parents weren't looking, Kevin took the last piece of pancake off his 8-year-old sister's plate. Predictably, she started crying and yelling. When his mom and dad confronted the boy, he exploded into a tirade about how his sister had started it. Kevin's dad finally ordered him to his room until he could act his age. Kevin did go to his room and spent most of the day there. By the time his father realized that his son hadn't done his chores, it was too late to do them before the family had to leave for an outing.

Procrastinators use any excuse they can think of to put off their work. Their behavior is different from that of youngsters who delay tasks until the last minute because the pressure of the deadline helps them focus on getting the job done. Procrastinators want to avoid the task entirely; they don't want to deal with a situation they dislike or feel incompetent to tackle.

Procrastination results from inadequate skills, a lack of self-confidence, and parental pressure to meet unrealistic expectations. The best way to stop procrastinators from wasting energy is to help them analyze assignments, chores, or activities so they can check to see that they have the necessary skills for the task. (See chapter 8.)

The Excuse-Maker

Behaviors:	Invents excuses, rationalizes, lies, blames others or events
Thinking Style:	*Internal messages:* "I'm no good." "I'm lazy." "I can't do it." "I'm lost." *External messages:* "It's someone else's fault." "It wasn't my fault, things just happened."
Feelings:	Hopeless, inadequate, overwhelmed, resentful, helpless

Excuse-makers always have a reason for incomplete or poorly executed assignments. This is the child who fails to do her laundry because "there isn't enough detergent". Instead of checking the cupboard for surplus supplies or asking a parent, she truly believes she's off the hook.

These youngsters justify their behavior with such finesse that parents are often knocked off balance. Excuse-makers rationalize their behavior because they fear the real reason they don't follow through is their basic worthlessness and inadequacy. This perception—or misperception—is too difficult for children to consciously accept about themselves, so they reject it. But they must still explain why they have failed, so they invent excuses, explanations, or lies. Usually their excuses are illogical and hard to follow.

Jim, age 14, was supposed to take out the trash every Tuesday night, for Wednesday morning pick-up. One Tuesday evening when his father, Alex, asked him whether he had done the task, Jim replied, "I didn't because the weatherman said we're going to have strong winds and rain tonight. I'll do it tomorrow morning before school." On the one hand this sounded logical. On the other, it smelled like an excuse. Alex made the difficult decision of giving Jim the benefit of the doubt.

When Alex pulled into the garage the next evening, however, he began seething. The trash was still piled high in the driveway. Jim knew he had blown it the second his dad walked in the door. Trying to come up with a quick excuse, Jim breathlessly explained, "My alarm broke. I overslept. I woke up late and then I remembered I promised to walk my girlfriend to school. There was no time to take out the trash and make it to school on time." Alex knew that if he told Jim the excuse was irresponsible, a fight would follow.

Lots of parental energy gets spent in excuse-making behavior, which parents unwittingly set in motion. As Jim saw it, he didn't have to worry about his chores until his dad questioned him about them. Because Alex hadn't established an accountability system for his son (see chapter 9), Jim suffered no consequences if he failed to take out the trash. He was free to wait for his father to remind him about it, and then free to ignore the reminder.

Even when an excuse-maker completes a task, it is rarely done well because the child does not put in the necessary time and effort. She relies on her excuses to bail herself out of the responsibility to complete a task to a certain standard. When Dolores told Kim, age 12, to clean the kitchen counters in preparation for Thanksgiving while she was at work, she returned to find dried cleanser all over the counter and floor. Dolores yelled at her daughter for the mess she had made, but

Kim shouted, "It's not my fault! I wiped up the cleanser when it was wet. There must be something wrong with the cleanser."

Kim felt that cleaning the counters the way her mom wanted it done was an overwhelming job, and she resented the very thought of having to do it. So Kim tackled the task and proceeded to do the fastest, sloppiest job she thought she could get away with.

Had Dolores sat down with Kim and explained how to clean the tiles and grout, the girl would have seen the task as a step-by-step process she could handle. In addition, the discussion of the task would have helped Kim to feel more a part of the process of deciding how the job should be done. She would have been able to give her input.

As students, excuse-makers are disorganized, slow workers who create rationalizations to justify incomplete or sloppy work. Their behavior is a cover for their lack of organizational and fundamental academic skills. They are easily discouraged and feel inadequate because they truly don't understand how to earn good grades. They often lack the basic skills necessary to be successful students, as in Jamie's case.

Jamie's teacher began each day by asking the fifth-grade class to get out their math homework and turn to the proper page in the math book. She had been making the request every day since school started a month earlier. By walking up and down the aisle, she could quickly see who had completed the homework and who had not.

Day after day, Jamie would look in her backpack for her assignment. More often than not, it was missing or incomplete. Mrs. Flint would ask, "Jamie, where's your homework?" Jamie would reply:

- "I forgot it at home."

- "My mother didn't give it back to me after she checked it."

- "I didn't understand how to do it."
- "I went out with my family last night and didn't have time to do it."
- "I was sick and my mom told me I didn't have to do it."

The list of excuses that "prevented" Jamie from showing or doing her work went on forever. She used these same replies to explain incomplete assignments in other subjects as well. Finally, Mrs. Flint requested a conference with Jamie and her parents. She told them, "I think Jamie is really bright but because she doesn't do her work, she isn't learning the skills she needs to get good grades this year or next."

Jamie's parents could see how frustrated the teacher was with their daughter, and they understood the feeling well. This was the third year they had attended such a conference, and they were becoming impatient and alarmed. Sandra and Mark had provided an appropriate place for Jamie to do her homework and had set up an hour and half daily for the task. But Jamie spent the time daydreaming. She rationalized that the assignments were stupid and made excuses about why she didn't need to finish them until the appointed time slipped by.

Mark had noticed, however, that whenever an assignment included drawing, Jamie completed it willingly and handed it in on time. "If you can remember those assignments and do them well, why can't you finish your other assignments?" he asked his daughter in frustration.

The art assignments were easy for Jamie because she understood how to do them and derived satisfaction from them. Jamie remembered assignments she felt comfortable with and forgot those that intimidated her.

This youngster did not know how to deal with frustration. As soon as she felt inadequate or uncertain about how to do a task, she would become frustrated. To deal with this feeling, she escaped by daydreaming. That prevented her from learning the very skills that caused her problems. With practice, however, Jamie was able to recognize that when she found herself doodling on her schoolwork she was starting to feel frustrated because she was unsure about how to do it. She learned to ask for help early, before her frustration grew so uncomfortable that she needed to escape. Chapter 9 delves into the common problem of how to deal with frustration.

When an excuse-maker believes he can't do what is expected of him at home or at school, he won't even try; he doesn't know how to proceed. Instead, he uses his energy to find reasons why the poor performance was not his fault. Excuse-making children often feel lost. When asked to explain their behavior, they fabricate explanations to avoid feeling overwhelmed and inadequate. Parents and teachers keep this circle of defeat going by reiterating their expectations instead of determining why the child feels inadequate and avoids the work in the first place. Often the adults fail to check whether the child possesses the skills to do the job. (See chapter 8 for information on taking a skills inventory.)

Unfortunately, excuse-making prevents children from getting the feedback they need to learn skills and discover their own strengths and weaknesses. Youngsters who participate in school get the attention necessary for their development. Since excuse-makers don't participate, they feel like outsiders. They further rationalize their isolation by claiming that school is boring and unimportant. The excuse-maker's unmet need for attention often produces disruptive behavior that can be extreme.

Kelly, age 13, was always getting out of his seat, even though the classroom rule was to raise one's hand and ask permission. He would intentionally wait until the teacher was lecturing, then give the other students a chance to watch the "show" between him and the teacher. When Mr. Combs told Kelly to sit down or asked him why he was out of his seat, Kelly had an excuse handy to challenge the rules. "I broke my pencil and have to sharpen it right away so I can take notes for the test tomorrow," he'd say, or "I need to get a ruler so I can underline neatly."

Kelly paid a price for this inappropriate attention-getting behavior; it only further alienated him from his classmates. They laughed at his antics, but they didn't want to include him in their groups for class projects because they knew he wouldn't do his share of the work. Additionally, because the teacher saw Kelly as a disruptive influence in the class time and time again, he subconsciously labeled him a kid who didn't care. Consequently, Mr. Combs' expectations for Kelly plummeted.

Kelly's acting-out problems stemmed from a deficiency in basic academic skills. Upon determining in therapy that Kelly had a spontaneous temperament, his parents and I realized how difficult it was for him to sit still in class. Ever since he had entered school, he'd thought more about how to get out of his seat and move around than about learning. I suggested to Kelly and his parents that he get involved with organized athletic programs to channel his physical energy. Also his parents hired a tutor to teach him how to take class notes and to improve his writing skills, areas of deficiency that were contributing to his problems.

Excuse-makers find it difficult to take responsibility and be accountable for their actions. Hopelessness, inadequacy, and a sense of being overwhelmed are emotions worth exploring with these children. Excuse-makers think that the system, whether in school or in the family, doesn't support them. They don't know how to take control of their lives and make the system work for them. To help excuse-makers, parents and teachers must define their responsibilities clearly, have an accountability system in place, and check to see that these children know how to do the tasks required of them. (See chapters 7, 8, and 9.)

The Master Manipulator

Behaviors:	Manipulates others; acts defensive, selfish, controlling
Thinking Style:	*Internal Messages:* "Life isn't fair." "No one cares about me." "I have to look out for me first." "I'll get back at them." *External messages:* "No one can tell me what to do." "You can't control me."
Feelings:	Insecure, powerless, inadequate, defective, resentful, vengeful, angry, helpless

Master manipulators want to be in control of their own lives. From their point of view, by following an authority figure's dictates they will sacrifice their personal needs and desires. They resist being told what to do and respond to their parents and other authority figures with anger, defensiveness, and resentment. Their behavior gives the impression that they don't need or want anything from others.

Underneath this false front, however, is a child who feels unloved and rejected, a child who believes the key people in his life—his parents—don't care about him. Since his parents won't meet the youngster's needs, he feels he is not obligated to care for them or be cooperative in return. Indeed, he believes he must look out only for himself. The child's resentment over his parents' power is expressed through underachievement—an attempt at revenge.

The parents of a master manipulator can be controlling and may frequently overuse their authority. These parents want their children to follow directives without question. Unfortunately, they ignore their children's thoughts, feelings, wants, and desires. When the children retaliate, parents use more oppressive forms of control, starting a vicious cycle of dominance and revenge.

Shana's case was extreme. A 15-year-old sophomore, she had a history of good grades in elementary school. Throughout her freshman year of high school, however, her performance slipped steadily, reaching an all-time low the first quarter of her sophomore year. When Shana and her parents came in for counseling, they were pitted against each other in a desperate struggle. How had their relationship deteriorated so badly? The battle being fought was over who controlled Shana's life.

During her freshman year Shana's mom, Dixie, went back to work full-time as a newscaster. While Shana was always responsible for some household chores, now she was "forced" to make dinner every night. Shana resented the new order. She told her parents, "It's not fair that I have to get stuck making dinner. Why should I have to do it just because you wanted to go back to work? You can't make me!"

Rather than trying to find a workable solution, Dixie replied with equal anger, "Oh yes you will! There is no reason why you can't do it! You waste too much time on the phone anyway!"

Shana responded to her mom's authoritarian demands by manipulating the situation. She would start dinner late, forget to prepare some of the items on Dixie's menu, accidentally burn the meal, or overseason the food in hopes that her mom would realize this new arrangement was untenable. But Dixie reacted by severely curtailing Shana's use of the phone so she would "pay more attention to her cooking."

Seeing that she was losing the battle, Shana then started to lie. The teenager told her mother she was getting math help from one of her friends after school on Mondays and Wednesdays so she wouldn't be home in time to cook dinner. Dixie responded by requiring Shana to be responsible for dinner anyway.

Loss of phone privileges interfered with Shana's social life, and she became resentful and angry. She felt increasingly isolated from her friends since she didn't have time to keep up with the latest gossip. As a result, instead of doing her homework, she started using the phone right after school when her mother was at work. Consequently, Shana was failing two of her classes. This was her retaliation. Her parents responded to Shana's poor grades by further restricting her activities.

By the time this embattled family came in for counseling, all of Shana's privileges had been withdrawn: no phone, TV, dating, or outings with friends. Predictably, Shana resented such extensive restrictions and told her parents, "You're treating me like a criminal. That's cruel and unfair." Her parents responded with more threats. They warned that they wouldn't allow her to enroll in driver's training if she didn't obey. The war was on. Shana ran away to a friend's house. Sobbing wildly when her parents came to get her, she threatened suicide. Frightened and angry, Shana's parents grounded their daughter for a month.

To Shana, getting the grades her parents wanted only meant giving in to their demands that she fulfill all of their expectations. But for Shana to agree with her parents meant they had won the war and she had lost control over her own life. Shana was manipulating her parents into a power struggle that was destructive to all of them. Indeed, her life became so unbearable that she turned to drinking to escape from the pressure and tension at home.

Shana's sad example demonstrates how far master manipulators can go to avoid feeling powerless. Since Shana really didn't want to go through with suicide, the only control she felt she could exert was to do poorly in school and to drink. Fortunately, during family therapy sessions, Shana was able to become a part of the decision-making that affected her life.

Since Shana's parents recognized that their restrictions on her activities were causing her to be more disobedient, they were ready to try a new way of parenting. They learned to listen to Shana's point of view by asking questions to make sure they knew how she felt and what caused her to feel a certain way. Then they used a decision-making model (see chapter 9) to help define the problem, seek alternatives, and discuss consequences. In this way Shana knew what part of each decision she had control over and what part was a family standard that was not negotiable. This prevented parent and teenager from making decisions that were arbitrary and emotionally laden and would therefore cause a power struggle between them. The use of shared decision-making returned to Shana some sense of control in her life and made her feel more empowered as a person.

Master manipulators also exert control over their lives by figuring out the rules of the game in any situation, from surviving in school, to getting people to do what they want. They play on people's emotions to get their way. Master manipulators are great at singing the blues to teachers if their assignments are late or if they fail a test. They may exhibit such sincerity or innocence that their instructors make an exception to their usual policies. These youngsters are terrific at making deals that people can't refuse.

Cindy, age 16, refused to spend the time it took to do well in school. She was satisfied with her C average and didn't understand why her mother got so upset about grades. Janice, a single parent, was enrolled in a doctorate program that met at night twice a week. With school, a job, and three kids, Janice routinely felt overburdened. In order to cope and keep life moving smoothly, she ran a pretty tight ship.

Cindy, sensing how much her mom needed help, started fixing dinner without being asked. However, whenever Janice got angry about Cindy's poor grades, the youngster replied, "I'm doing my best. Helping out at home takes time, too." Janice instantly felt guilty and anxious for criticizing Cindy. She viewed her child as a good daughter and an ally whose help she didn't want to relinquish. Janice even began to wonder if maybe C's were all Cindy was capable of obtaining.

Having rendered Janice guilty, Cindy no longer had to deal with any pressure about her grades. She wrestled control from her mother and used her time as she saw fit.

This situation was told to me years later by Cindy, now 25. She had come for therapy because she was unhappy and depressed. When we reviewed her behavior as a 16-year-old, she recognized how costly her manipulations actually were. She now saw that she had passed up an opportunity to discover her strengths and weaknesses in an environment that supported her growth. She no longer had the structure of school and teachers who were available as safety nets to identify and impart the skills necessary for success; it was much more difficult for an adult to have a variety of opportunities to learn about herself.

Often the master manipulator's need to set his own agenda occurs at the expense of other family members. Jason, age nine, and his family were in counseling because of the constant bickering between him and his six-year-old sister, Patti. His mom, Gwen, a teacher, and his father, Billy, a land developer, were busy and active. Every day Gwen made Jason watch his sister for an hour while she caught up on grading papers. The boy hated baby-sitting because it took away most of his playtime. When he complained to his mom about the unfairness of the situation, she told him, "Sorry, that's just the way it's going to be."

Jason felt his mom didn't care about him or his desire to play with his friends, so why should he care about his sister? Consequently, he became increasingly selfish and argumentative. When the family went on vacation to Yellowstone National Park, he and his sister were told to bring some toys for the long drive. Jason couldn't be bothered with packing because he was playing with his friends until the last minute. In the excitement of leaving, his mother forgot to check on his packing.

Once the family was on the road, Jason quickly became bored. He started taking Patti's toys and inventing his own games with them. When Patti saw him mistreating her favorite doll, she screamed, "Stop it!" In an effort to appease Jason, Gwen warned him to play with Patti's toys nicely, but she never mentioned that since he chose to "forget" his own toys, he had no right to his sister's. Predictably, within a half hour, Patti was crying again. This time Billy stopped the car and threatened, "If you touch any of Patti's toys or say anything for the rest of the trip, you're going to be in serious trouble!"

Jason expressed his resentment at his father by kicking Patti when his parents couldn't see. Each time she yelled, Jason claimed Patti was lying.

Had Jason's family known about effective communication, they might have listened to each other's feelings and then responded supportively. Gwen and Billy might even have understood the rejection and abandonment behind their son's manipulative ways.

Master manipulators usually have low expectations of themselves because high standards make them feel out of control. They are defensive and may use emotional outbursts to discourage parents or teachers from confronting them. They know just when to bring home an isolated A to relieve and deflect parental concern about overall performance. Because of all the time and energy these children invest in order to be in control of their lives, they may fail to master other age-appropriate developmental skills.

Unfortunately, master manipulators feel the most powerful when they are in the throes of manipulating a situation. It is hard for these children to accept others' authority without a negative reaction because they have never felt truly accepted for themselves. Any perceived control by others makes them feel even more diminished and inadequate. They tend to hear all directives as criticism, which makes them feel defective. They think they are doing fine because they have found ways to live within the rules. But at the same time they think rules are stupid and never truly understand how discipline can enhance their personal gifts and goals.

Dealing with a master manipulator takes time, energy, and continuous effort. As a result, parents tend either to overreact in a controlling way or to ignore them. Unfortunately, this inconsistency encourages the master manipulator to try anything to get what he wants. Setting up an accountability system (see chapters 8 and 9) that outlines a child's responsibilities, the consequences he will experience if he fails to live up to them, and the privileges he will experience if he does, lets the master manipulator know that his behavior, not his manipulativeness, will determine his lifestyle.

The Dropout

Behaviors:	Quits, withdraws
Thinking Style:	*Internal messages:* "I don't fit in." "I can't do it their way." "I don't care." *External messages:* "I'm leaving." "This situation is stupid."
Feelings:	Defective, rejected, alienated, different, helpless, depressed, despairing, hopeless

The dropout is the maverick of underachievers. Often a sensitive and original loner, he recognizes early on that his uniqueness is at odds with the family or school system. Like a creative artist in a totalitarian political regime, eventually he simply defects rather than conform. Indeed, conformity feels like death to his sense of self. He quits and walks away instead.

These children want to leave a structured environment because they can't find enough acceptance and support within it. They believe dropping out will free them, but such an act is difficult. So dropouts subconsciously set up events to make it appear as if the system is rejecting them, when in fact it is they who reject the system.

Authority figures become angered and confused by these youngsters because they can't relate to dropping out of a system. Their point of reference is to succeed by working within the system. To authority figures dropping out means giving up and admitting failure, something that is alien to their thinking.

Tina had been in kindergarten for only three months when the teacher called Denise, her mother, to report problems with the girl's social interactions. Whenever Tina had to share a toy, she erupted in a tantrum. Similar behavior occurred at home. Denise had established a family rule that all of her children should share their toys. But Tina had a favorite doll that she didn't want to share with her older sister, Kate. Whenever Kate took the doll, Tina screamed. Denise would reprimand Tina for being selfish. While this mother wanted to teach her daughters to share, she had denied Tina's need to have a special doll of her own. Tina felt helpless to make her mom understand her need and desire.

Ms. Miller told Denise that whenever Tina had these outbursts, she was going to seat the child in a "time-out chair" to help her control her behavior. Unfortunately, the teacher's strategy only exacerbated Tina's situation. The youngster's anger at being given a time-out masked her true feelings of helplessness. Once again she felt no one cared about what she wanted. When she recognized that her teacher was going to keep disciplining her, she withdrew into depression. In effect, Tina dropped out of class participation. To her that meant she no longer had to live by the class rules. Neither Denise nor Ms. Miller could ascertain why it was so difficult for Tina to share a toy. As this behavior continued, Denise's confusion turned to anger. She felt frustrated at being unable to reach her daughter.

Denise was the youngest child of a large family and had often felt powerless to have her own way. Her attempt to ensure equal attention and worth for all her children motivated her to enforce her rule about sharing. Balancing the needs and desires of each family member was Denise's real issue. Through counseling, Denise recognized that sharing and respect for each other's personal property could coexist with a sense of family. Denise started to hold family meetings and restructured how the family made decisions to support both the individual members and the family as a whole. In chapter 6 you will learn how to use this skill.

When children lack a sense of love, acceptance, and support, they distance themselves emotionally. This further prevents them from learning socialization skills and developing morally. Children who drop out are at high risk for developing antisocial and destructive behavior patterns. Mood swings and depression are often characteristics of the dropout's personality. Even though the external defensive attitude is one of not caring, inside these children care very much and feel hurt, despairing, and rejected.

Dave, a 16-year-old high school junior, had a history of incomplete assignments and poor attendance. Throughout his freshman and sophomore years, he was warned that if his performance didn't improve, he would be assigned to continuation school. Failing three out of the four classes in which he had enrolled, he was transferred the second semester of his junior year.

Dave pretended he didn't care, when in actuality he felt helpless and hopeless. After the first two weeks of continuation school, he felt alienated from the new academic setting; once again he felt unaccepted and unacknowledged. Consequently, he started putting in more hours at his part-time job at a surf shop, where he molded surfboards. The teenager liked working with his hands and felt comfortable in the shop because he was left alone to do his work. In addition, he was paid for every surfboard he completed.

For Dave, the work environment didn't require that he fit in. Even though continuation school had minimal structure, Dave felt threatened by having to accommodate any large system. He dropped out of school. His parents became furious and gave him an ultimatum: if he did not return to school he had to find somewhere else to live. Dave resented his parents' attitude, so he moved in with an older brother who was frequently absent from his apartment.

In leaving the system for fear of being unable to survive, Dave actually set up a worse situation for himself. This adolescent was unready for the responsibility of being on his own. He was at great risk of becoming involved with alcohol, drugs, and antisocial behavior—maladaptive coping strategies for the anger that surfaces when people feel separated from support systems and denied acceptance. Because he never felt part of the system, he had no sense of connection, alliance, or respect for it. Is it any surprise that dropouts often brea laws?

Dave's parents recognized that he was stuck in his life. They wanted him to come back home but feared that if they extended the invitation they would have to accept their son's standard of living. At the same time, Dave realized how lonely he was. On the suggestion of a friend, Dave's parents came to counseling to clarify their thoughts and feelings and to decide what to do. They approached Dave and told him that they no longer had preconceived expectations for him. Then they listed the things they would provide as parents if he came home, and they told him he would be responsible for certain tasks to help keep the family functioning. Another stipulation was that he join them in counseling so they could discover realistic expectations for him.

By treating their son as an equal and needed part of the family by giving him tasks, the parents helped Dave recognize that he belonged. Most importantly, he saw that being a dropout didn't bring him the rewards he thought it would. As counseling progressed, Dave's self-worth developed, as did his participation in family and school.

Children like Dave only feel safe, secure, and accepted in an environment that makes sense to them. They must be able to understand where they fit into the system. In order to help them bridge the gap between recognizing their uniqueness and knowing how the system can support them, it's important to first communicate effectively with them. Then, through participation in family meetings (see chapter 6), they can become a part of shared decision-making whenever possible. They need to understand that the system, whether at home or school, can value them.

Identifying the type of underachieving behavior pattern that your child exhibits will help you understand his thinking and feelings. This in turn helps you understand what causes his behavior. As a parent you react to this behavior in your own way. In the next chapter you will see how your child reacts to parental behaviors that are intended to help him be successful—but often backfire.

Chapter Five

Do You Recognize Yourself?

Parenting Practices That Backfire

Most overachieving parents want their family life to align with behaviors that support achievement. The ideal family for achievement-oriented parents would consist of active children who are self-reliant, cooperative, and productive. The children would respect their parents and recognize that their advice is valuable because it shows the youngsters how to achieve and make their lives "work." Of course, such kids would willingly adopt their parents' values and be dedicated to trying as hard as possible to follow through with their goals enthusiastically.

Is your family living this fantasy? Probably not. That's because your child doesn't hold the same expectations you do. Whereas you may wish that your youngster accepted your version of important values and societal standards, he may seek proof that you love him for himself, whether or not he can meet those standards. He resists your values in order to discover who *he* is and to see if that person is still lovable to you.

All overachieving parents hope to instill positive values in their families. I often encounter the following belief: "Our family is active, successful, and supportive of one another." The way the parents try to get these values actualized is interpreted differently by each member of the family. The underachieving child feels pressured to perform so she will fit in with the rest of the family. She is likely to interpret the parental values to mean, "In order to be accepted in this family, I must achieve."

We all want to be good parents and to nurture values that will lead to our children's success. Paradoxically, however, the harder we push our kids to succeed, the more likely they are to fail. It's difficult for us to recognize that what we think are good parenting practices often make our kids feel put down, intimidated, or discounted. This, in turn, causes the very underachieving behaviors that are so frustrating to us in the first place.

If you want to break this cycle, your first step is to take a good look at your parenting practices and the messages behind them. Do you recognize yourself in any of the descriptions this chapter?

"If One Activity Is Good, Ten Must Be Better"

To counter the fear that their children might be lazy, achieving parents often enroll their youngsters in all kinds of activities. But children resist participating in activities chosen for them. They are unlikely to show any enthusiasm or gratitude for the parents' plans and certainly will not put in the effort required to perform well if they haven't chosen the activity themselves.

Becky, age 12, participated in gymnastics for five years but stopped when she developed a knee problem. Even though Becky was a cheerleader at her middle school and a Girl Scout junior leader, her mother, Tisha, insisted that she replace gymnastics with another activity. Becky didn't want to. She liked the attention she was starting to get from boys at school, and she wanted enough free time to be able to talk on the phone after school. Tisha threatened to take away her daughter's phone privileges if she didn't select an activity by the end of the week. To Tisha phone use was nonproductive time.

When Becky failed to think of a new activity, Tisha took the initiative and enrolled her on the swim team. She campaigned for Becky's participation with the reminder that swimming would keep Becky slim—an important motivator. Becky knew how relentless her mother could be, and after Tisha's pep talk she thought maybe swimming would be okay after all, so she halfheartedly joined the team.

After several weeks, Becky wanted off the team. She was tired of the coach yelling at her to "move faster, you can do it" and her mother telling her that she needed to put more effort into her swimming because she was a talented athlete. The constant pressure on Becky to live up to others' expectations started taking its toll. Her grades dropped; she was tired all the time; and her enthusiasm for cheerleading and scouts waned.

Becky felt discouraged and powerless. Moreover, she was angry and frustrated with her mother, who wouldn't listen to or understand her feelings. To take more control of her life, Becky started flirting with and teasing the boys in her class. She enjoyed the power she felt seeing their reactions. When the principal called Tisha to tell her that Becky had been caught making out with a boy behind the handball court at recess, Tisha was horrified.

In this self-destructive way, Becky was trying to tell her mother that she wanted to make decisions for herself. Tisha's demand for Becky to stay overly active caused Becky to rebel, despite her mother's original intent of keeping Becky involved in constructive activities.

During a therapy session, I asked Tisha to list her expectations for Becky. I also asked Becky to list goals for herself. Starting with the items that were common on both lists, we worked together to write a plan to accomplish the goals. In this way, mother and daughter were learning the process of shared decision making. When Becky recognized that Tisha was listening to her input, her rebellious attitude faded. Using this process we set up standards for Becky such as maintaining a certain grade-point average, being involved in an afterschool activity, and working on a personal goal that was designed to provide a growth experience. Becky then was able to decide how she was going to fulfill these standards. It was clear to Becky that her privileges, such as social activities, were linked to maintaining the standards. She chose to stay in cheerleading, she made a study schedule, and she decided to take art lessons on Saturday mornings as a personal growth activity.

Parents may also keep their children "too busy" out of their own needs. Activities provide a supervised, safe setting while parents are at work or otherwise occupied. Robin, age 11, was constantly on the go. Mondays and Wednesdays she had ballet after school. Tuesdays were reserved for Girls Scouts. Spanish class met Thursdays. Fridays, she took flute lessons.

Although Robin was a bright, talented girl, this whirlwind of activities overwhelmed her and prevented her from doing well in any one of them. She always felt out of breath and disorganized. Whenever her mother, Lucy, lectured her about trying harder, Robin became depressed. She just didn't know how to handle all the demands on her. She repeatedly asked her mother to let her drop some of the activities. But each time she mentioned it, Lucy delivered another lecture on the value of the experience.

Lucy was constantly busy with work and community politics. When I asked her how Robin was doing, she admitted, "not well." As we talked, it became obvious that Lucy needed Robin to remain fully occupied so Lucy wouldn't feel guilty about being gone all the time. Robin's many activities might have been enriching had there been fewer of them, but as things stood, they functioned as Robin's baby-sitters. After our discussion,

Lucy realized she had to come to terms with her guilt and make choices that supported Robin's needs.

No matter how good you think an activity is for your youngster, don't railroad him into it. You need to truly listen to what your youngster is saying about his interests and dislikes. Be alert to what draws his attention naturally and use that as the starting point for activities he will enjoy. Then observe his interest level as he becomes involved. Finally, you can help him set realistic goals regarding what he wants to gain from the new experience. (See chapter 8.)

"I Am Responsible for My Child's Success"

You know how essential it is to teach responsibility to your children. To develop this important trait, most parents keep track of their children's progress in school and elsewhere. Monitoring your youngsters' activities allows you to make sure they are following through with their commitments. It also helps you see where and when you are needed as a parent. But when you take responsibility for your child's performance—in other words, when monitoring turns into policing—trouble usually develops. Monitoring changes into policing when the responsibility for your child's behavior shifts from the child to you.

Laura, a single parent, started an exciting new job that required her to work longer hours than her previous employment. Although she loved the challenge, she felt the pressure of trying to stay in charge at home and work. Since she was no longer available to make sure her 11-year-old twin daughters did their homework right after school, she never knew whether they completed it. Whenever she asked Heather and Dana if they were finished, they responded "Yes" automatically. The girls were pleased with their newfound "alone time" but at the same time uncertain whether their mom really cared about them as much as she used to. When report cards came out, both girls had lower grades than ever before. Laura was furious and told her girls how irresponsible she thought they were and how disappointed she was in them.

Laura then started to make Heather and Dana show her their homework every evening. Since she felt guilty for being unavailable to oversee their progress, she was quick to criticize their work when she did look at it. She wanted them to be responsible for completing the assignment, but she also wanted them to do the best work *she* thought they were capable of. If they did well, she believed she could justify the many hours her new job required, and escape her guilty feelings.

For their part, Heather and Dana began to dread "check-in time." Laura invariably found fault with their work and insisted they weren't trying hard enough. They felt frustrated and hurt because their mother no longer seemed to appreciate their efforts. When she made them redo assignments, fighting often erupted. In time, Laura became more invested in her daughters' schoolwork than the girls were themselves. Unfortunately, Heather and Dana understood neither their mom's intent to make them responsible nor her ambivalence about the long hours her new job required. Instead, they reacted to Laura's harsh criticism by resisting it.

Both girls told me in a therapy session that they felt their mom had changed: "We can't talk to her about our personal problems like we used to," they complained. "We don't like her being angry all the time. We feel like we can't please her anymore." Laura, meanwhile, couldn't understand the distance that had developed between her and her daughters. She thought she was only doing what she needed to do in order for them to learn to be responsible.

In chapter 8 you will find an explanation of the homework accountability system that allowed Laura to put the responsibility back on her daughters' shoulders where it belonged. Both mother and daughters had definable responsibilities in the homework system, and preset consequences were specified for any poor choices the girls made. This allowed Laura to interact with her children in many more ways than a policeman.

Monitoring involves checking with your child to make sure he has fulfilled the responsibilities that the two of you have specified in advance. If your child fails to perform, you're satisfied with giving a reminder or a warning of a clear consequence if the behavior recurs. Your youngster makes choices about his behavior.

When you police your child, in contrast, you are after only one outcome—you want a task done your way. You're willing to take the responsibility away from your youngster to make sure your goal is reached. Shifting from a strategy that supports your youngster in becoming responsible to one that denies him responsibility for his achievements only causes him to resist. Resistance can come in many forms, including avoiding work, doing a sloppy job, being disrespectful, and defying you outright.

When children don't have a clear idea of their responsibilities, it's all too easy for them to become irresponsible. Had Laura explained the time requirements of her new job, defined her standards to her girls in terms of her concern for them, checked to see if they knew the tasks involved in getting their homework done, and then developed an accountability system (see chapters 8 and 9), Heather and Dana would have been in charge of their own performance.

"Let Me Tell You How to Do It"

As parents we all want to convey words of wisdom to our children in the hope that they will learn from our experiences and avoid the mistakes we've made. We hope that by sharing our experiences, we will be able to make their lives easier, happier, and more successful. But when we lecture our kids, give pep talks, or tell stories about our past, we can turn them off. These one-way conversations ignore their reality and assert our own.

"I'll Tell You What to Do"

Lectures and monologues are given with the unspoken premise that the lecturer knows more than the lectured. Underachievers' frustrating behaviors can provoke hours of lecturing from achieving parents. What parent can resist delivering a diatribe on the need for organization, the consequences of procrastination, or the perils of lying? But because lecturing parents rarely come up for air, they give their children no chance to respond. Consequently, the lecturer cannot know whether the speech was on target.

Most children readily admit that they never listen to lectures. Instead, they are thinking:

- "Mom's overreacting again!"
- "Dad's so stupid. He doesn't even know what he's saying!"
- "I wish I didn't live here."
- "I hate her!"

Lectures usually follow wrongdoing. Most of the time, children know they've made a mistake, but they may have difficulty owning up to it and facing the consequences. A lecture only makes it more difficult for kids to admit their mistakes and learn from them. To do so would mean losing even more face. It's one thing for your child to admit he is wrong, but to have to admit that his parents are right at the same time can be asking too much of him.

Kerry, age 10, found himself in just such a predicament when he convinced his parents that he and his 7-year-old brother, Scott, were old enough to stay home alone while his parents went grocery shopping. The parents stated the rules before leaving: "Don't answer the door, cook, or roughhouse together."

As soon as their parents left, however, Scott started bugging Kerry while he was playing a computer game. "Knock it off!" Kerry yelled. But Scott continued hitting a computer key and running away. Before long the boys got into a shoving match and the computer monitor fell off the desk. Luckily only the brightness knob broke. But now Kerry would have to confess that he had roughhoused.

When Kerry heard the car in the driveway, he started down the stairs to tell his mother and father what had happened. But Scott ran out and related his version first. Kerry reached the kitchen the moment his parents did and didn't have a chance to say a word before the lecture began. At first Kerry tried to interrupt to apologize. He wanted to tell them he knew he was wrong to shove Scott. But when they started saying how he was always irresponsible, the boy seethed inside.

Had this youngster been allowed to explain what had happened, admit his mistake, apologize, and willingly take any consequence his parents deemed necessary, the incident could have become an opportunity to develop a new level of trust within the family. Instead, Kerry wouldn't even think about telling the truth in the future because his parents demonstrated how little they cared about his side of the story.

"You Can Do It"

Observing parents watch their kids is a study in anxiety. Whether we are attending a school play, seeing our kids through confirmation or bar mitzvah, or rooting for them on the playing field, we are focused on them to the exclusion of all else. Not only do we want them to succeed, we also insist that they do their very best. Before any event, we find ourselves giving our children pep talks.

Like lectures, pep talks are a form of one-way communication. Your intent is to give your child enough confidence to dispel any self-doubt. You let her know you think she can do the task at hand. However, for the overachieving parent, pep talks often turn into a prescription for action and, worse yet, an expression of expectations. As Penny drove her daughter Jane to the school district spelling bee, she said, "I know you'll be able to win tonight. Just remember to take a deep breath before starting to spell the word. I'm sure you'll get first place!"

Because you have experienced the exhilaration of winning, you would like your child to enjoy the pleasure too. Indeed, you may want so much for your child to experience success that you may be unrealistic about her skill or commitment level. You may even lose track of your boundaries and see yourself in your child, forgetting that she is an entirely different human being from you.

It was 11-year-old Geoff's idea to join the soccer team, and his mother, Debra, was delighted. A single parent, Debra was worried about her son because he hadn't seemed to care about anything since her divorce two years earlier. When she attended the first game of the season, she recognized that Geoff was a good athlete, but she felt he exhibited the same unfocused behavior she had observed at home. "He is just not aggressive or involved enough," she thought. "Perhaps giving him some confidence and letting him know what I think he can do might make him more successful and turn things around."

Debra's "confidence building" came in the form of pep talks in the car on the way to the weekly games. "I know you can run faster to kick the ball to the goalie more often. All you need to do is pay attention and keep your eyes on the ball. Then you'll do great." But after a couple of weeks, Debra saw no change in Geoff's performance. Moreover, it became increasingly difficult to get the boy to practice every day.

Debra didn't realize that her pep talks were really prescriptions for performance, not words of encouragement. To make matters worse, her expectations and instructions differed from the coach's. Frank, the coach, also recognized Geoff as a good athlete, but he knew the boy was an inexperienced soccer player. He had Geoff practice specific drills during each game to work on a variety of skills. Geoff couldn't please both his mother and the coach, so he became confused and anxious. He couldn't think his way through his increasingly threatened feelings, so he began to withdraw from the situation that provoked them.

Debra was unaware that her pep talk directives were at odds with the coach's development plan for Geoff. She was also unaware how invested she was in her son's performance. Her pep talks were intended more to elicit the behavior she saw as desirable than to bolster the boy's self-confidence. They made the soccer games hers instead of Geoff's. How did this family resolve its conflict? After yet another game in which Debra saw little improvement, she asked in frustration, "Geoff, don't you care about being a good player?"

"I want to be a good player for the coach," Geoff replied. Debra was stunned. It finally dawned on her that her son wanted the coach's approval, not hers. She also realized how important it was for him to have a positive relationship with his coach since he seldom saw his father. Her pep talks were dividing Geoff's loyalty. Once she stopped issuing directives and started encouraging him, she saw that he increased his effort.

Not all pep talks are damaging. Appropriate pep talks need to be positive, affirming statements that support a child's spirit more than a specific behavior or achievement. The best pep talks enhance the youngster's belief in himself. They reassure him he is okay, no matter what the outcome of a specific event may be. Some examples of appropriate pep talks are:

- "I would vote for you for president of your class. Your speech really states what you want to do. And the way you practiced, it sounds great! Go get 'em!"

- "I know you are going to do your personal best on your test. You studied so hard!"

- "Do your personal best—I'm excited to see what you will do!"

- "I know you have a great deal of inner strength. Pull it together and go for it!"

"When I Was Your Age..."

Many of the common social adjustment problems children encounter, such as making friends, getting along with parents, learning to share with siblings, navigating through school, and interacting with the opposite sex, are universal to the human experience. The conflicts played out around these core issues, however, vary from one generation to the next.

Sharing your own experiences can be a valuable teaching tool. The following are some useful examples:

- "I made a mistake dropping out of college when I was 20. Going to night school to finish my degree and working during the day was difficult."

- "I dated a girl I felt sorry for and didn't really like her. I didn't want to hurt her feelings by ending the relationship. But later I realized I hurt her more by not being truthful."

- "I couldn't decide what I wanted to be when I went into college. Even after the second year I was unsure. I knew I had to figure it out so I could declare a major. I signed on as an ordinary seaman on a petroleum tanker for six months. Everyone thought I was crazy but it made me grow up. That's when I decided to be a teacher."

- "When I was in high school, I was so in love with a guy who was a freshman in college. He was the most important person in my life. I would go see him on weekends, making a long drive each week. When the relationship ended and I didn't have any girlfriends left, I knew how dependent I was on that one person to make me happy. From that experience, I learned to balance my life and make *me* the most important person in my life."

The best kind of storytelling brings comfort, wonder, and a sense of connection. It's really about the listener more than the teller. In this kind of story, relating your experiences is only appropriate if you ask your child first if she would like to hear what you have to say and if you can make the experience relevant to her own. Often, however, our stories are a not-so-subtle attempt at influencing our kids or telling them what to do. You'll know that inappropriate storytelling is going on when you hear yourself saying:

- "Here is how I handled a similar situation when I was your age..."
- "What's the big deal?"
- "You think *you* have it rough..."
- "Kids today have it so easy compared to when I was young!"

In these instances, the angry, hurt child within you competes with the angry, hurt child standing before you whom you don't know how to handle. When you try to impress your children with the value of your experiences, you assume that only you know how to make things turn out right. Even if you begin by sharing mistakes you've made, chances are you'll finish with a story of your success.

As with other forms of one-way communication, your child is expected to listen to your story without interacting. This prevents him from discussing how (or even if) your story applies to him. An opportunity to share common experiences and closeness disappears. Instead, by holding your own life up as the model, you can cause your youngster to feel discounted and insecure. Moreover, to protect himself from feeling criticized, he is apt to rebel against your standards.

Danny, age 17, turned to his father for advice when he found himself in a bind. He and his friend Louie were both on the school basketball team. That meant no drinking or drugs and maintaining a C average. Danny had been like a big brother to Louie ever since Louie's dad died in an automobile accident the year before. One night, Louie went to a party without

Danny. There, he tried cocaine and marijuana; he was afraid the other kids would think he was uncool if he said no. From that moment on, Louie was hooked on cocaine. He resented Danny's lecturing about how wrong it was and how it could get him kicked off the basketball team. Drug use could spell the end of his chances for a college sports scholarship.

Danny became scared for his friend, who was using drugs more often each week, and he went to his father for advice. His dad said, "When I was your age, I had a similar problem. One of the guys was drinking. To save the whole team from being disgraced, I told my baseball coach. Although my teammates never spoke to me again, I still think I did the right thing. Go tell the coach, son." Danny couldn't relate to his father's story. Didn't his dad understand that Louie was susceptible to drug use because of his pain over his father's death? Danny knew that if Louie was kicked off the team, he would never get off drugs. Never before had Danny felt so alienated from his father and so alone. "Doesn't he care about my best friend?" Danny wondered. His respect for his dad died that day.

Had Danny's father told his story and then asked his son what he thought about it, Danny would have had an opportunity to explore the applications to his own situation. This would have helped Danny clarify his thoughts and feelings. He might have come up with a solution that would work for him.

Appropriate storytelling is about consciously recognizing the challenges your child faces growing up in today's world. It's *not* about unconsciously trying to get your son or daughter to be impressed by the difficulties *you* faced as a child.

"I Want My Child to Be Number One"

When your youngster shows an interest in an activity, you want to support her being the best she can be. But often for achieving parents "the best" isn't a description of definable behaviors but rather an attitude. No matter what the child accomplishes, it still may not fill the bill. Maybe if she tries harder, we think, she will be able to do even better. In our desire to see constant improvement, to test the limits, or to find out what is "the best," we put a great deal of pressure on our child. She never gets a sense of when her effort is enough.

Janet, age 12, was tops on her gymnastics team. Ever since she was 7, gymnastics had been the center of her life. Her mother, Shelly, went to all her practices and meets. She would analyze Janet's performance during the drive home. When Janet did well, her mom was happy and talkative. She even made special desserts for dinner those nights. But when Janet didn't work as hard as Shelly thought she should, Shelly turned a cold shoulder. Predictably, being ignored made Janet feel there must be something wrong with her. She feared that no one loved her. She felt so much pressure to perform that she started making beginner's mistakes.

Then Janet fell off the horizontal bar at a meet and sprained her ankle badly. Although Shelly hadn't uttered a word, Janet sensed that her mother felt she had fallen on purpose. For the next two weeks, Shelly was short-tempered with a daughter who had to use crutches. When Janet went into a state of depression and refused to get out of bed, this family came in for therapy.

Shelly's approach to motivating her daughter actually caused Janet to become insecure about herself. She felt her mom's love was conditional—Shelly loved her only if she achieved to her high expectations. The emotional turmoil Janet experienced because of her mom's attitude prevented her from concentrating on her gymnastics and achieving at her ability level.

In therapy, we separated Shelly's expectations for Janet from Janet's goals for herself. This mother realized that the anger and frustration she felt toward Janet reflected her mistaken belief that she was responsible for Janet's success. She felt she was doing her part but that Janet wasn't.

Shelly now recognized that Janet was the one who had to decide what she wanted from gymnastics. Janet decided to return to gymnastics and wrote down the goals she wanted to accomplish by the end of the season. With my support, Shelly stopped going to all of Janet's practices and used the time to start a physical fitness routine of her own.

Failure to meet performance expectations is an emotionally laden situation for parents and children alike. Often parents assume that their child is performing poorly on purpose when in fact the child is still struggling to master new skills. Unfortunately, such parents interpret their youngster's expectable setbacks as personal affronts.

While it's true that your child may well fail in order to get back at you, it is important to guard against creating the potential for such a reaction by withdrawing your love or making your love conditional on performance.

"Why Can't Johnny Get an A? His Sister Does"

Sibling rivalry can make the home a battlefield. It angers parents, causes tension in the family, and damages children's self-esteem. When your child senses that his brother or sister is getting more of your attention or love than he is, he feels devastated and rejected. His pain is so intense that he may become emotionally distant from family members and can adopt a defensive attitude, which in turn alienates others.

Sibling rivalry can be created or deepened by the overachieving/underachieving dynamic in families. When parents are focused on achievement as a measure of their children's and their own success, they give their achieving children more recognition and attention. They want all of their children to be successful according to their standards. Consciously or subconsciously they may compare one child to another with remarks such as:

- "Your sister gets A's on her report card. Why can't you?"

- "Why can't you follow the rules like your younger brother?"

- "If you tried as hard as your sister, you'd succeed."

These can exacerbate existing jealousies. Children are quick to recognize when parental love, attention, and material possessions are distributed according to achievement. They become shrewd household monitors of how Mom and Dad mete out discipline, household chores, privileges, and praise. When children perceive an inequality, they feel inadequate and become jealous and angry with the favored brother or sister.

When I was working with Marta, age 12, she complained that her mother, Marjorie, always yelled at her and compared her to Jessica, her 16-year-old sister. While this was an exaggeration, other family members observed that when Marjorie talked to Jessica her voice was calm, but when she talked to Marta, even about neutral topics, she spoke faster and sounded tense.

In defending herself, Marjorie explained, "Jessica causes me few problems, so I don't have to be on guard when conversing with her. But Marta is never doing what she's supposed to. I'm always ready for an argument from her."

Marta's feelings of self-worth, meanwhile, were abysmal. Marjorie was constantly asking her, "Why can't you do things right, like your sister? Why do you always have to start problems?" Marta's hatred for Jessica was intensified by their mother's habit of bringing Jessica presents. In revenge Marta wore Jessica's clothes without permission. Of course this made the 16-year-old furious, and the fights went on and on.

Marta's defense: "It isn't fair that Jessica always gets new clothes." Marjorie's response: "If you got good grades like your sister, then maybe I would consider buying you things, too!"

The family came in for counseling when the fights between the girls became physical. During the session, it was revealing to see Marjorie side with Jessica, and her husband, Lou, side with Marta. As the family members shared their feelings and expectations about each other, it became obvious that Marjorie favored Jessica because the older girl was an achiever like herself. She couldn't understand why Marta got poor grades and was rebellious, especially since Marta was so intelligent. Marjorie's desire for Marta to be like her and Jessica made Marta feel excluded. She knew she was different.

Lou, meanwhile, saw this special bonding between Jessica and his wife and therefore campaigned on Marta's behalf. He told Marjorie that she was too harsh with the younger girl and was expecting too much from her. That had the effect of further alienating Marjorie from Marta. Her husband's support for Marta caused her to feel inadequate as a parent to Marta, whereas she felt successful as a parent to Jessica. This intensified her bond with her older daughter. That, in turn, only strained the relationship between the sisters even more.

Above all, Marta wanted to have a relationship with her mother without having to be like her. Many of the techniques you will learn in chapters 6, 7, and 9 helped these family members appreciate each other's differences. As Marjorie, Lou, Jessica, and Marta started looking for and acknowledging each person's strengths, the rivalry between the girls diminished.

Labeling children is another form of comparison that leads to sibling rivalry. When I was a teacher, I let my students know what areas of strength I observed in each of them. During parent conferences, I discussed these and asked if the parents saw the same positive qualities I had observed. The limited view some parents had of their children often amazed me. For example, when I mentioned to one parent that her daughter was an excellent writer, she said, "Mary isn't the one with writing talent. It's her sister, Peggy." Peggy was labeled the writer in the family and that was that.

If you are unsure whether you label your children, observe what you say about them to others. That's when you reveal your biases. Many parents make this mistake. In fact, in my own family, we labeled one daughter "the athlete" and the other "the brain." In truth, each was athletic and intelligent, but because of the labeling, each played out the assigned role and under-achieved in the other area. At the time, my husband and I thought we were helping both of them to have an area in which they excelled. We thought it would diminish the rivalry between them. But by labeling them, we were actually increasing the competition between them and limiting their opportunities.

Underachievers suffer from the negative image they must labor under and the accolades their brothers and sisters enjoy. It's difficult for a child to compete in the same arena as a sibling who has already been dubbed a success. The risk is too great that the underachiever's accomplishments will go unacknowl-edged or—worse yet—that he will be compared to the successful sibling. The underachiever's anger at being labeled is inevitably directed toward the object of his jealousy, his sibling. It is less threatening for a child to express rage at a sibling than a parent. However, in the final analysis, the child is angry with his parents because they are not providing the love or attention he wants. Intense sibling rivalry lets you know your children lack the support and encouragement they sorely need.

"If They Know It Makes Me Happy, Maybe They Will Do It Again"

Praise can be both an encouragement and a manipulation. It is encouraging when used to support what your child has already recognized as important to her. Bonnie loved to make kites. When her parents saw her latest original design, they exclaimed,

"That kite is terrific! You really know how to make special kites!" Bonnie beamed when she heard the praise because she was proud of her talents too. The parental comment was a reflection of what Bonnie already felt and knew but hadn't voiced herself. With the acknowledgment from her parents she was encouraged to keep designing new and different kites.

Praise becomes a manipulation when used to reinforce specific behaviors that parents find desirable. Underachieving children are suspect of praise because they interpret it as judgment. In fact, manipulative praise is veiled criticism. When you say:

- "Wow, what a good boy you are!"
- "I'm so proud that you got an A on your math test!"
- "You did a great job! You did just like I told you."
- "You played like a superstar. See, practicing that extra half an hour paid off."
- "I'm so happy when you get on the honor roll at school."

the message your child receives loud and clear is: "When you do something I value, you are a worthwhile person." Praise is a form of control that says, "I will give you love and attention if you perform to my expectations."

Praise tells the child how he is supposed to act in order to get approval from you. But praise is based on your judgment (and not your child's) of how he should perform. Unfortunately, parental praise so influences kids that they often do whatever they must to receive it. This narrows their field of experience.

When Abbie, aged 15, received an A on her essay at school, her mother, Charlene, praised her success. "You did a number one job on your paper. I'm so proud of you!" Charlene's intent was to reinforce a standard of achievement in the hope that Abbie would repeat her effort on the next assignment and get another A. In truth, however, this teen had written the essay at the last minute and was surprised by the grade. Because her mother never asked her how *she* felt about the grade, all Abbie learned from getting an A was that she wouldn't have to try any harder on her next essay. After all, her parents and her teacher were pleased with her hurried effort.

Charlene's praise made it easy for her daughter to avoid the next step in her academic career. Abbie was a talented writer who could have gone on to a career in journalism or freelance writing. Had she been acknowledged for her essay and then encouraged to seek out the next creative possibility for growth, she might not have allowed her writing ability to plateau. Abbie knew she could do even better than that essay, but she wondered why she should try when her mother and teacher were so thrilled with her work already. Such complacency is an under-achieving attitude.

Praise can also make children dependent on others' opinions, giving them the idea that they are only worthwhile when they please others. When children become addicted to praise, they wait to see whether they get it to decide how they should feel. They don't trust their own ability to decide if their efforts were good enough.

Parental praise is especially confusing for underachievers. They know that most of the time their parents are disappointed in them. When their parents suddenly express pleasure, these youngsters wonder if the praise means that their behavior has suddenly become acceptable. They're unsure about what they have to do to keep their folks happy.

Indeed, many underachievers feel guilty about unexpected and unusual attention, as if they were undeserving. Their self-esteem is so low that they can't allow themselves to truly hear the praise; they can't recognize themselves as capable of any success. Moreover, if they happen to hit the jackpot and receive praise, they feel pressured to continue the approved behavior. They now fear their parents will expect it. Underachievers lack the self-confidence to believe they can change permanently and positively. Doing something right once in a while is quite differ-ent from hitting the mark consistently. If you praise your child excessively, you can easily activate or reactivate underachieving attitudes and behaviors.

Carrie praised her 16-year-old daughter, Tammy, sincerely. "I'm so proud of you," she would say. "You did a perfect job on your term paper." Or, "I'm so happy that you got an A. It's terrific." Or, "You are such a wonderful daughter to get an honorable mention in the art fair."

Tammy never acknowledged these comments. In fact, Carrie began to notice that whenever she praised Tammy, her daughter would provoke her by defiantly talking back to her to such a degree that within a day or two, she'd feel obligated to take away one of Tammy's privileges. Tammy couldn't handle the pressure of being "good," so she would misbehave to get back into the familiar but negative pattern. Now she felt comfortable knowing what to expect. Once lauded, however, she feared disappointing Carrie and herself by being unable to keep up the praiseworthy behavior.

If your praise is really a trap to limit your child's behavior or impose your goals upon her, the strategy will backfire repeatedly. Praise only has value if your child also values what you are acknowledging. When Carrie started making statements that were based on Tammy's specific positive, observable, and measurable behaviors, Tammy was able to accept the approval because it was based on fact, not her mother's judgment. For example, when Carrie said, "I noticed that last week you finished your homework before talking on the phone. You really showed self-discipline," Tammy replied, "I'm trying to get all my work done before I watch TV or use the phone so I can relax and not feel guilty." Tammy could identify with her mother's comments because she valued her behavior too.

"Father Knows Best!"

Underachievers feel that parents and other authority figures such as teachers, coaches, and scout leaders control their lives. They may react to their loss of autonomy with fear, anger, and resentment. Authority figures, in turn, respond by becoming defensive and increasing the control rather than determining what caused the child's reaction in the first place. Children are not conscious of their motivations, but parents and authority figures, if they are sensitive, can be. Such sensitivity is a prerequisite for working with underachieving kids.

One of my young clients, Lynn, hated her father—for good reason. The man was an insensitive brute. Whenever Lynn was upset, he would make fun of her feelings and tell her to stop being such a "wimp." It didn't matter what was bothering her. When she studied for a test and got a D, her father put her down with, "D is for Dumbo! Not much happening between those ears, is there, kid?" When she finally got angry and started yelling at him for being a "jerk," he reprimanded her for talking disrespectfully to him. Moreover, it infuriated Lynn when her father laughed at her at the dinner table, because he gave her siblings the message that she was fair game. Lynn's father refused to come for counseling.

During therapy, I helped Lynn distinguish appropriate and inappropriate uses of authority. I also helped her reduce her emotional reactivity to her father's comments. When her dad made comments that hurt her feelings, she made the following clear statement: "When you call me names it hurts my feelings." At first he tried to tease her about her new response. But, she countered with "You are hurting my feelings right now." Because Lynn expressed herself neutrally, her father recognized that his comments weren't having the predictable angry effect. Through practice, Lynn was able to distance herself from her father's remarks but still clearly state how she felt. Because of her more assertive response to his remarks, Lynn's dad slowly stopped making them.

Underachievers perceive their parents using authority arbitrarily and unfairly. Unfortunately, as in Lynn's case, this perception may be correct. Parents who abuse their parental authority make their kids feel inadequate. Children lack the skills to handle problems with power figures. Some under-achievers respond to authoritarian parents by overtly confronting them, leading to intense power struggles in which both kids and parents invariably lose. Other underachievers learn to avoid overt interactions with authoritarian parents, but they strike covertly. These youngsters see resistance as the easi-est way to get parents and teachers off their backs. They express their balkiness with the attitude, "I won't do it!" Parents become frustrated and angry when children say "I can't do it," because they don't know how to determine whether "can't" really means "won't."

Bo wanted to sign up for driver's training in order to get his license as soon as he turned 16 in six months. He dreaded ask-ing his father for the money for the course because he knew his dad would belittle him. But he was desperate enough to set aside his misgivings. "Dad," Bo asked one evening, "I'd like to start driver's…"

"If you think you are going to sign up for driver's training with your grades and your attitude, you are greatly mistaken!" his father, Paul, snapped back. After Bo endured an hour's lec-ture about his shortcomings, Paul agreed to reconsider if Bo "changed his attitude and improved his grades."

Paul's tirade didn't help Bo because the demands were too vague. The teenager felt frustrated. But since he desperately wanted his driver's license, he tried being nice. He even started doing his homework regularly. However, if Bo didn't jump when Paul made a demand, the boy would hear the same lec-ture about "maybe you don't really want your license." This became a no-win situation for Bo. He had no idea what his father wanted from him and he resented being "jacked around." Finally, Bo was so furious with the way his dad took advantage of him, that he shouted, "Screw the license. I don't give a damn anymore!"

The rift between Bo and his father was unnecessary. If Paul had clearly stated the requirements for his son to get his license and identified who was responsible for what, the needs of both would have been met. (See chapters 8 and 9.)

Now that you have a better grasp of why your child underachieves, it's time to do something about it. In Part II, you will learn concrete ways to support your youngster in changing his behavior.

Part II

Helping Yourself / Helping Your Child

Chapter Six

Creating a Family Structure

All children need to be part of a family structure that provides love, acceptance, respect, safety, and security. These fundamentals will support your child as he grows into a competent, happy, and successful adult. As his needs are met, your youngster develops an alliance with and allegiance to the family. Consequently, he adopts your value system because he sees that it works. The natural adjunct to his allegiance is his ability and willingness to return to other family members the love, acceptance, and respect bestowed upon him.

However, if the child's needs are unacknowledged or unmet, he will withdraw emotionally from his parents and transfer his loyalty to any individual or group that he perceives will meet his needs. For underachieving children this usually means an association with other underachievers. While your youngster perceives these relationships as free of expectations and demands, they do reinforce his negative attitudes, which in turn support his underachieving behaviors and intensify his alienation from the family. These friendships provide a sense of belonging, so essential to every human being. The allegiance to the friend or group, and hence the influence from that association, easily become more powerful than the bond with the family.

If there is a positive family structure, your child will naturally seek the company of its members. He will want to participate in family activities because he knows they will be fun and satisfying.

The family structure is a management system you develop to meet the everyday challenges of life. To have a nurturing, successful family, the structure must incorporate ways to meet each family member's essential needs. First let's explore your developing child's needs. Next, we'll discuss ways to structure your family management style to fulfill those needs.

Your Child's Essential Needs

Abraham Maslow was a psychologist who studied highly successful people and developed the theory that human needs and motivations can be placed on a hierarchy or ladder. The lowest rungs of the motivational hierarchy are physiological needs such as food and shelter. Once these needs are met, an individual must secure a certain amount of control over his environment, creating a sense of safety and security. Only when basic needs are satisfied will the individual become involved in his social environment.

Social interactions with family, friends, teammates, and others satisfy the child's need to belong and be loved. Self-esteem, the next rung on the ladder, develops as a consequence of successful interactions with others. This is how your child learns about himself. A well-developed self-esteem is the foundation from which the maturing child reaches his highest potential. Maslow calls those who are able to express their highest self and help others reach their potential "self-actualizing" individuals.

What follows is my adaptation of Maslow's theory to the needs of underachieving children and their families.

Children Need to Feel Loved

Only when your child experiences love can she appreciate her positive qualities and grow to love herself. This in turn provides her with self-confidence to take the necessary risks on the journey to success. The ability to love or even appreciate one's self underlies the child's expectations of success in her endeavors. It permeates all aspects of her life and affects her relations with herself and others. A child can only live what she understands and has experienced.

In chapter 7 we will concentrate on verbal communication. But words are not the only way to say "I love you." Nonverbal communication—a pat on the back, a smile, the tone of voice, a squeeze of the hand—are also powerful. For example, when Judy noticed Jackie slouch through the door, her eyes red and puffy, she knew without asking that Jackie had lost the election for team captain. Judy put her arm around her daughter and gave her a hug. Jackie started crying and held on to her mom. Words were unnecessary for Judy to show her love and allow her daughter to grieve.

Showing appreciation is another form of love. It says "I value you." When Lester came home from work he was pleasantly surprised to find his 15-year-old son George had straightened up the workbench after fixing his bicycle. He jumped out of his car and went straight to George to say, "Thank you so much for cleaning up the workbench. I really appreciate it. Somehow I never found the time to do it. The mess always made me feel guilty when I looked at it. Now it won't nag at me anymore! You did a great job!"

George glowed as he replied, "Well, I figured I would clean it since I use the workbench, too."

When Lester showed his appreciation for George, the boy felt like a competent and valued contributor to the family. This is a wonderful example of how people can turn their lives around. When George and his folks first came to therapy, the boy had just been kicked out of school for failing grades and drug use. George had been an underachiever who had dropped out of the system because he felt no one cared.

As achieving parents, your schedule may be full and your child may be well aware of how busy you are. Since you never seem to have enough time, the way you choose to spend your hours tells your child what is important to you. When you sit and talk with your youngster or share activities that are important and of interest to her, you also express love. Your involvement lets her know you are glad she is in your life and that you enjoy being with her.

Tim had poor grades and was having a difficult time following through with his household chores, but he was a whiz at computer games. Tim's father, Michael, recognizing that most of his interactions with his son were negative, needed to find a positive way to relate to his youngster while applying the skills they had learned in counseling. Michael had never allowed himself time to play computer games before, but now he felt this would be a good opportunity for him to relate to his son. In the spirit of sharing his son's interests, he put the competitive aspect of playing games in check and proceeded to have fun with Tim.

At first Tim was mistrustful of this new interaction. After all, his father had only criticized his interest in computer games before. But as he saw Michael enjoying himself, he recognized that this wasn't a "one-shot deal" and he let his guard down. The feeling of love and trust that developed between father and son made it possible for them to change other areas of their relationship. Tim was now able to receive math help from his father without feeling criticized. Seeing that he could improve his failing math grade made him confident about himself and he put more effort into all his classes. Also, Tim now looked forward to doing the lawn and other chores with his father since he was at ease with him. This became the time for Tim to try out his jokes. Michael enjoyed this part of his son he had never seen before. Spending time with your child is a gift for both of you.

Children Need to Be Accepted for Who They Are

To be accurate, your perception of your child must include his vision of himself. You need to support him in taking the risks necessary to discover who he is. It is through self-selected, creative risk-taking that children develop confidence in their own self-worth. Your role is to allow your child to explore the possibilities by choosing activities that interest him. In that way, the activity becomes the child's own. Once he has mastered such a challenge, he will observe and appreciate who he has become as a result of the experience.

Ira, age 15, and his family were working on shifting the focus within the family from Ira's wrongdoing to his skills and interests. In the past, Ira's helpless and hopeless attitude about his life had severed him from his classmates and from school activities. He just never seemed to care or to have the energy to get beyond watching TV or playing games on his computer. His parents, Phyllis and Jon, decided to use the evening meal as an opportunity to become more involved in their children's lives. First, they made a commitment to be home for dinner. Then, they decided to discuss family issues and world events. As they asked Ira for his opinions, he slowly started to come out of his shell and participate. Indeed, over time, Phyllis and Jon found that making the effort share dinnertime and the communication skills they had learned in therapy (see chapter 7) had really paid off.

One evening Ira shared what had been discussed in his social studies class. As he talked about apartheid, his parents could appreciate how strongly he felt about the unfairness of politics in South Africa. They listened and asked questions and were delighted to see the depth of his interest. "I want to make a difference in the world," Ira said, "by making people more aware of the problem in South Africa."

Over the next few days he enlisted a couple of new buddies to help with his cause. The boys met and decided that they were going to silk-screen T-shirts with slogans that mirrored their political philosophy and sell them at the school carnival the following month. Although Phyllis and Jon were thrilled with their son's enthusiasm, given his previous attitude they were concerned that he might fail to follow through. They decided to approach his request to front him the money for the T-shirts as if it were a business deal. As in any venture, Ira's "lenders" wanted a business plan. So Ira and his parents sat down to create one. This gave the family an opportunity to practice more new skills. Together they analyzed the task (see Chapter 8). Each person was assigned a role in getting Ira's project off the ground. Since Phyllis and Jon recognized the importance of their son doing "his thing," they choose only to provide the money and the encouragement. Jon stated at the end of the meeting that he was impressed that Ira was willing to risk entering this venture. He knew it would be a learning experience for everyone involved.

Jon's statement reduced the pressure to succeed that had sabotaged Ira in the past. Now the focus was not so much on the end result as on the value of the experience. Nevertheless, at times it was difficult for Jon and Phyllis to remain mum, especially when they saw some of the mistakes Ira and his friends made. It was hard to walk into the garage day after day and see the mess from the project. But Ira was involved, active, and excited. To his parents' delight, his excitement energized him enough to motivate him to tackle his schoolwork. Moreover, as a result of the attention he received for selling the anti-apartheid T-shirts, Ira felt more in charge of his life than ever before. That realization greatly enhanced his self-image. Now he believed that he could make things happen.

Kids need to follow their interests, and parents need to support them in doing so with a minimum of interference. Accepting your child for who he is also means judiciously withholding your prejudices and fears, especially when a new project excites him. All too often, underachieving children like Ira hesitate to take on any project, no matter how small, for fear of failure and disapproval. If you add your own fears you inadvertently feed your youngster's self-doubt.

Randolph, age 18, exhibited the behavior, feelings, and thinking style of a master manipulator. In therapy his father, Rick, realized how often he condemned Randolph's interests as dangerous or useless. Rick's effort to control Randolph had always stifled the boy's enthusiasm to try new things. It also encouraged him to manipulate others to get his needs met. This behavior grew out of Randolph's belief that his father didn't care about him.

During our fifth therapy session, Randolph brought up the fact that he wanted to be a commercial pilot and to start flying lessons. Rick began to discourage Randolph, as he had many times before. "Flying is an insecure profession," he said. "Once you became a pilot, there's no room for advancement. The stress levels are too high, and being a pilot doesn't provide a lifestyle conducive to family life." Rick was getting ready to deliver his next barrage, when he stopped himself and said, "I'm doing it again! I didn't ask Randolph about his feelings!"

Randolph agreed. Then he said, "Dad, when you give me reasons why being a pilot is a poor decision, it makes me doubt myself and think that I'm stupid to want to fly. Yet inside myself, I know I want to be a pilot. I feel so alienated from you, Dad, because I don't fit in with your values."

After hearing how he was undermining Randolph's self-confidence, Rick said, "Okay, I'm willing to support your desire to be a pilot. Let's see what we can work out." It was decided that Rick would match each dollar Randolph earned toward flying lessons. But perhaps most importantly, Rick mentally and emotionally accepted that he didn't have the power or the desire to force his son to live by his own view of life.

If you want your children to fulfill your ambitions, chances are you haven't realized your own dreams. You might think that it's too late for you to fulfill that special dream because you are so entrenched with your successful career now. Consciously or subconsciously, though, you may be pushing your child to live out you own unmet ambitions.

Pat, an unfulfilled artist, was delighted when she first recognized that her son, Collin (now 19) had artistic talent. She was determined to give him a good background in art and enrolled him in afterschool art lessons several days a week. While Collin enjoyed the art classes, which he had taken for the last six years, he really loved building things. But whenever he talked about civil engineering, Pat carried on about how he was wasting great artistic talent. Pat's constant preaching put him at odds with his own vision of himself as an engineer. Soon his ambivalence became so great that it paralyzed his ability to decide what classes to take and which major to declare in college. Sadly, he took joy in neither his art nor his engineering classes, performing poorly in both.

While in therapy, Pat recognized and accepted that her desire for Collin to be an artist represented her own unfulfilled dream. When she took the responsibility for her own vision by taking art classes at night, Collin was released from the pressure to live his mother's vision. He took a semester off school to think things out and returned as an engineering student.

Our youngsters look to us to help define who they are. We must reflect back a clear image of what we see, an image undistorted by our fears and ambitions.

Children Need to Be Respected

Your child, though young, inexperienced, and in need of guidance, is still a separate person from you. She has her own ideas, feelings, desires, and needs that are as valid as any adult's. Consequently, you must take into consideration your youngster's point of view about the decisions that affect her life.

Unfortunately, many parents think their child should automatically respect them because they provide for her. But respect is earned through caring about one another's needs and feelings. Parents of underachievers may fail to show respect to their children, often because of their frustrations with their child's behavior. Yet they expect their child to automatically respect the parents.

Nevertheless, no matter what the situation, respect can always be a part of your interaction. Even when you are reprimanding or make a request of your child, you can show respect. When scolding, for example, you must be clear about the specific behaviors you want your child to change and the new behavior you want her to develop. Make your wishes known in simple statements devoid of any criticism, putdowns, or anger, such as:

- "Johnny, I don't want you to put your feet on the coffee table because it makes marks on the wood. If you need to put your feet up, sit in the chair that has the ottoman."

- "Melissa, you've been leaving your makeup on the counter when you use the bathroom in the morning. I want you to put your makeup in the drawer, so the bathroom is neat."

- "Stewart, you are leaving dirty dishes on the counter when you have your afterschool snack. I want you to rinse the dishes and put them in the dishwasher."

Because you are communicating respectfully, without criticism or anger, you will usually succeed in getting your child to respond. It may take some time, but as your youngster feels more and more a part of the family, she will take others into consideration.

If your child is not at that point of cooperation yet, move to a statement that specifies a consequence for the child's failing to comply.

- "Marty, you left your bike in the driveway three times this week. I want you to put it in the garage when you come home from playing with your friends. If you can't do this, I will not allow you to use your bike for the next day."

- "Sara, you have been on the phone for an hour. I asked you twice before to limit your telephone calls to 15 minutes each so others may use the phone. If you go over that limit from now on, you will lose phone privileges for 24 hours."

- "Keri, you didn't put away the computer disks after you finished playing games with your friend yesterday, as you promised. I had to do it before I could get to my work. You know that I need the computer for my business. If you forget to clean up my work area again, I won't let you use the computer for a week."

Your tone will enable your child to hear what you say without feeling put down, defensive, or wrong—emotions that alienate him from you.

You can respectfully make a request of your child and ask for cooperation within the same communication. Just as in reprimanding, you need to establish consequences if a simple request doesn't work:

- "Jack, I see you're in the middle of a TV program. I need for you to take out the trash before nine o'clock. When can I count on you doing it?"

- "Barbara, we've run out of towels, and that's your job. We need clean ones before eight o'clock. When will you load them into the washer?"

- "Bill, my car needs to be washed before Saturday. When will you be able to do it?"

Showing respect for your child's activities is important to him. You may consider the TV program unimportant but your youngster may have an entirely different opinion about it. Expecting him to automatically respond to your demand to shut off the set while he's in the middle of a favorite show instead of allowing him to wait for the commercial or the final scene can be misuse of your authority. Likewise, with any activity in which your child is involved, whether it be homework, talking on the phone, or visiting with one of his friends, arbitrarily interrupting and demanding an immediate action is disrespectful.

Children Need to Feel Safe and Secure

Daily and weekly routines that your kids can count on create a predictable and safe home environment. The Luken family discovered the importance of this principle the hard way. When Rosalind, a newly appointed member of the city planning commission, came in to therapy with her husband, Lee, a partner in a manufacturing company, they both complained that their family was out of control. Both parents described their children, 13-year-old Pauline and 11-year-old Justin, as disrespectful and selfish. Both were poor students.

When I asked the kids during the first family session how they felt about being part of the family, Pauline said, "My parents are never home. We never know what time dinner is or if Mom is going to cook."

"I can never count on my parents because something always comes up at work," Justin chimed in. "They don't care about me, so I don't care about them!" Both kids said that their parents hadn't followed through on promises and had failed to show up at appointed times.

"My mom once forgot to pick me up from play practice," Pauline complained.

"And I didn't get to play in the soccer playoffs because my dad was late to take me to the game," Justin added.

Rosalind responded angrily to these accusations. "You make it sound as if it's all our fault," she yelled. "Why can't the two of you make dinner once in a while, or make an effort to find your own rides?"

Even though Rosalind's comment was made to defend herself from the onslaught of her children's anger, it did have merit. In later sessions we used the point brought out in this statement—"Who is responsible for what?"—to determine what family changes needed to be made.

In therapy, Lee and Rosalind realized their children were unready to handle the amount of unsupervised time they were faced with. The Luken family needed a management plan that included assigned responsibilities for each member. They also developed a homework accountability system (see Chapter 8). Lee and Rosalind agreed to restrict the number of nights they were out, and they made sure that one parent was home every evening.

As this family worked in therapy, they recognized the importance of following through with consequences. If parents don't follow through, children receive the message that they aren't important enough for mom and dad to take the time to discipline them. Children feel safe and cared for when parents set limits on their behavior. Parents create security when they clearly state and enforce family routines and discipline standards.

Children also feel safe when they know what to expect from parents. Inconsistent emotional behavior causes a child to be insecure. That was the root of Nancy's problems. Nancy, age 13, was afraid to bring her friends to the house because she could never predict when her dad, Ray, was going to be in one of his "moods." Ray, an investment banker, was often under pressure. When work was going well he was easygoing and fun to be with. But if business turned sour, he would overreact at Nancy's slightest infraction. His emotional tirades included name-calling and yelling. Nancy felt too embarrassed to have her friends see her father this way.

As a result of her dad's emotionally abusive behavior, Nancy sought solace and a false sense of security from boys at school. Preoccupied with her need for male attention, she began experimenting with sex.

When Nancy's parents discovered her sexual behavior, they were furious. While in therapy, Nancy explained to her parents that she hated coming home because she feared her dad would be in one of his moods. But during therapy Nancy also realized that she wasn't the cause of her dad's emotional outbursts. She had believed that some flaw within her had caused her father's verbal attacks.

Once Ray understood that Nancy's insecurity had caused her inappropriate behavior, he dedicated himself to dealing with his job-related frustration and anger differently. He had been putting pressure on himself by expecting accomplishments that were nearly impossible to achieve. Then he judged himself harshly when he failed to meet his lofty goals. Now, along with creating realistic weekly goals, Ray learned to identify his feelings and express them consistently instead of letting them build to the boiling point. He also worked out at a gym, listened to music, and did relaxation exercises to manage his anger.

As Nancy became more secure with her father, she no longer needed to gain a false sense of security from boys. She began inviting her girlfriends over to the house. That cured her loneliness. Because she felt safe with her father and her friends, she experienced a new zest for living. She joined student government and started taking karate lessons. These activities gave her a new sense of personal security.

The purpose of the family is to meet the needs of individual members within the family structure. As you create your family management style, keep in mind your underachieving children's basic needs: love, acceptance, respect, and security. When you design your model, ask yourself which needs will be supported by each of your management policies.

Family Management: Building Cooperation

Managing a family is similar to running a business. You need to have an organizational plan to accomplish your goals. Moreover, you have to set standards, make decisions about delegating responsibilities, and develop a system of accountability and evaluation while meeting the needs of each person. It's a tall order, but it's not impossible. Each family's management style is unique. The following are components of a management system that supports the needs of underachieving children and their families.

Setting Goals and Standards

It's vital for you to set standards that help your child grow and learn to be responsible as an individual, a family member, and a part of her society. Your child's understanding of responsibility is a simple equation: She receives privileges equal to her level of responsibility. In chapter 9, I will elaborate on this equation and help you set appropriate standards for your children.

My stepdaughters, for example, had to maintain a certain grade-point average appropriate to their ability level, perform particular household chores, participate in family activities, and be involved in extracurricular activities to develop their special talents and abilities in order to receive the privileges of driving, dating, and going to places and activities of their choice. We wrote out these standards and established consequences if the girls did not adhere to them.

This structure brings a sense of security and safety to children because they know what is expected of them and what will happen if they don't follow through.

My stepdaughter, Jill, for example, knew she had to maintain a certain grade-point average and have no grade below a C in order to drive the car we had given her. When we received a D notice from Jill's math teacher, she knew that she had to give her father the keys to the car until she brought home a signed note from the teacher stating her grade was at least a C. But even though she knew the rules in advance, Jill didn't believe we would take away her car. After all, she paid half the insurance on it. But we did follow through. Having to find a ride to school and even having to walk—a fate worse than death for a

16-year-old in Southern California—motivated her to be responsible for her grades. Never again did we get a D notice from school.

Creating a Joint Decision-Making Process

The Henry family was going through a major transition. Edith had decided to return to work as a psychiatric nurse after being a full-time mom for 16 years. Her 15-year-old daughter, Chris, adjusted quickly to her mom's new job. Her 11-year-old son, Ronnie, seemed nonchalant at first, but shortly after Edith started working, she received calls from Ronnie's teacher complaining that he was disruptive in class and had missed homework assignments. When husband Allen talked with their son about his behavior, he was surprised at Ronnie's defensive attitude. Edith and Allen were certain (and rightly so) that Ronnie was acting out because of Edith's employment. But they thought he would come around. Ronnie, however, continued to be remiss in his chores and homework, thereby provoking more criticism from his mom and dad.

When the Henry family came to me for help, Ronnie was feeling rejected by and alienated from his family. His hurt feelings caused an angry and rebellious attitude. I showed the Henry family a decision-making model (see chapter 9) that supports each person in expressing what he or she is thinking and feeling. As Ronnie listened to his parents, he realized that they did love and care about him, even though Edith couldn't give him the attention he was used to. By sitting down and working on some of the logistical problems that his mother's new job had created, Ronnie once more became part of the family.

Dinner had been a particularly problematic time for the family. Edith's job required her to work until 6:00 P.M., and she didn't arrive home until 6:45. Since Edith did the cooking, dinner wasn't served until 7:30 or later. The kids couldn't handle the wait, and snacked to excess before the meal. When Chris and Ronnie refused to finish their dinners, Edith became angry and frustrated. Telling them to stop snacking wasn't the solution because they truly were hungry and ready to eat dinner earlier than it could be ready. Instead, the family decided that Allen and one of the children would be responsible for cooking dinner. Chris and Ronnie would trade off helping their father. The odd man out would be responsible for the dishes. Allen would check for completeness in this task. Since Edith didn't leave for work until 10:00 A.M., she would shop for groceries, plan the menus, and leave recipes if necessary.

The Henrys decided to give this new plan a try for a month and then evaluate its success. By working with his father, Ronnie learned how to cook. That built his confidence to participate. Allen had become aware of the importance of teaching Ronnie the skills necessary to do the task, so the cooking lessons provided some great father-son time. Allen also worked with Ronnie every other night to make sure he developed an easy, effective system to wash the dishes thoroughly.

Since all four family members were part of the meal preparation, they became aware of the time and effort the task required and each appreciated the others' effort and unique flair. Dinnertime became a happily anticipated event because it truly was a joint family effort. As the bonding and trust deepened among family members, it became easier for all to share their thoughts and feelings about family and individual issues.

Increasingly, the Henrys were able to use this group focus to make decisions that affected the family. They jointly decided how they wanted to spend their vacations. They also designated Sunday afternoons as family activity time. They rotated the responsibility for coming up with an activity. As a group, they decided that the activity couldn't cost more than $15. Everyone needed to participate. They agreed to refrain from criticizing any planned activity and to give it an honest try. At Ronnie's suggestion the family went rock collecting in the local mountains. He was interested in geology, and the others had the opportunity to appreciate his new hobby. Edith planned a cookie-baking afternoon that everyone loved—especially at the end of the day. Allen had always wanted to try drawing, so he took the family to a beautiful lake and handed out paper and a variety of crayons, pastels, and pencils. He also brought along a surprise picnic. Chris planned a roller-skating outing. The Henrys also carved soap, made candles, and told stories. They planted an herb garden, built a bird feeder, and visited the art museum. Since all of the Henrys shared these activities, family members had an opportunity to respect each person's talents in a safe place. And most importantly, they had fun together.

Below are some guidelines to help you set up your own family meetings. This is an easy way to render decision-making a family process that bonds the family and builds loyalty to the family unit.

Family Meetings

Family meetings give parents and children the opportunity to express feelings and concerns in a supportive, constructive environment and to work together to make appropriate decisions.

Your roles are based on your family's particular needs. When you jointly decide how responsibilities will be apportioned, each person feels a part of the group. Through activities and decision-making at family meetings, parents and kids are acknowledged for who they are. Their special talents and strengths are recognized and utilized. In particular, this interaction provides an opportunity for the underachieving child to learn to act in new, more successful ways. The underachiever's realization that he contributes to the family and is valued for his uniqueness as a functioning member supports his changing self-image and his new expectations to achieve.

Adapt the following suggestions for family meetings to the specific needs of your family. If your child is too young to read or has a reading disability, then read the agenda to her or write for her the items she wants on the agenda. The point here is for children to participate at whatever level is appropriate for their age and ability.

Procedures

1. Family members rotate who is in charge of running the meeting. The leader creates an agenda that is posted for all to see the day before the meeting. (Everyone has the right to put items on the agenda.) He or she also follows through with time allotments for each agenda item if preset as a condition by the family.

2. Another family member is in charge of taking notes. These can then be used to draw up a written agreement if necessary.

3. A defined time period is established in advance and any items not covered are saved for a later meeting. Setting the length of a family meeting lets children know how long they need to pay attention. The age and attention span of your children will determine how long a meeting should be. The adage "short and sweet" is a good guideline. Observing how members manage the first meeting will help you decide about the next. With young children (6 to 8 years old), a 15- or 20-minute meeting may be all they can handle. Children 9 to 11 years old can easily participate for 30- to 45-minutes. For older children, an hour to an hour and a half is reasonable. The older the child, the more able he is to participate. The lengthened meeting will allow time for each member to contribute.

4. A written agreement is made for each appropriate item. Each person signs it.

5. One person is in charge of preparing refreshments to serve at the conclusion of the meeting.

Ground Rules for Family Meetings

1. No putdowns. If one is made, the person in charge makes sure the offender apologizes to the "offendee."

2. Each individual is responsible for making "I" statements. Anyone can ask for clarification if an "I" statement is not made. Chapter 7 will explain this concept.

3. All feelings stay within the meeting. Nothing expressed during the meeting is used against another person after the meeting. Feeling safe to express oneself is crucial to the establishment of trust.

4. Family members must stick to the subject at hand. If other concerns appear, they are put on the agenda for the next meeting.

5. All family members are responsible for previewing the agenda items so they can formulate a response in preparation for the meeting.

Written Agreements

A specific written agreement or plan of action is necessary to prevent any misunderstandings or "selective" forgetting that can result with a verbal agreement. Also, the process of writing down a plan and having all family members sign it allows for clarification and follow-up thinking. These steps ensure that decisions are livable and workable. Basically, the written agreement amounts to working the kinks out of the plan and making sure who is responsible for what.

1. State the agreement. Be specific.

2. List what needs to be done.

3. List the responsibility of each person involved. Do a task analysis and check for skill competency. (See chapter 8.)

4. Designate the date to reevaluate the plan. At that point, the family will assess what worked and what needs to be changed.

Family Culture

Family culture is a combination of management style and the family's traditions. Having traditions makes your child feel safe and secure because she can anticipate certain activities. It also develops a closeness within the family because it makes interactions special.

My husband, John, and I instituted a family birthday tradition. Each daughter was allowed to decide what she wanted to do on her birthday; the day was totally hers. But it was difficult for the other siblings to see so much focus on the birthday girl. More often than not, one of the other girls acted out in an attempt to get some attention. John came up with the perfect solution. Even though the birthday girl was the main event, our other two daughters also received a small gift. This helped all the girls look forward to the others' birthdays with excitement.

One of my clients told me about a tradition that was part of her family. Whenever a family member did something noteworthy, the achievement would be recognized during a special family dinner. The honoree picked the menu and was then served on a special red plate used only for these occasions.

When you think of your childhood, I'm sure some of your warmest feelings are associated with memories of family traditions. Whether it is caroling on Christmas Eve, going to the opening game of the baseball season, or enjoying certain foods at holidays, traditions provide a sense of consistency and well-being.

Setting up a family management system to meet your children's needs meets your needs, too. Parent and child alike need to feel loved, appreciated for who they are, respected, safe, and secure. A family management system helps you all to do so.

Chapter Seven

Putting the Relating in Communicating

Developing Trust Between Parent and Child

My clients have found that sharpening their communication skills dramatically improves their family life. Once you can all identify and express the feelings and thoughts you've bottled up, you're likely to feel an immense sense of freedom and possibility. When you're able to communicate with one another, your child won't feel stuck, and neither will you. You'll be in a much better position to work together once you know that you can talk to your youngster and he'll listen and respond.

It's best if you learn the skills in this chapter first and then teach them to your child and spouse. It's also advisable to learn one skill at a time and practice it until it becomes automatic. Then move on to the next. Before long, you'll have a repertoire of behaviors that will help your family to feel safe, loved, and accepted.

At first, you may find that using these skills feels a bit awkward. You may also find that family members won't immediately go along with the changes you want to initiate. But stick with it. Once your child sees that she can depend on your willingness to listen and respond (that it's not a passing phase), she'll be much more willing to change. After all, trying something new probably makes her feel inadequate and insecure. But when you consistently model a new skill, she'll learn it by sheer force of repetition. What's more, there's something in it for her, too. Once you're really communicating, your child will feel your love, and she'll be far less likely to sabotage herself with anger.

Interest your youngster in the process by enlisting her help. Invite her to be creative in finding ways to remind the whole family to use a particular skill. For example, when the Bellor family was learning to communicate their feelings, Ellen, age 6, drew a bear with a bubble coming out of his mouth that said, "I feel..." Posted in a prominent place on the refrigerator, the cartoon reminded the family to share their emotions.

Before we turn to the guidelines for good communication, let's consider the vital role it plays in our lives. Communication is the way we exchange information, come to a consensus, express thoughts and feelings, connect intimately with others, and explore ourselves. But it may also be used to cover up, deny, and defend against feelings that cause pain. Gossiping, lying, telling half-truths, omitting key facts, name-calling, silence, and defensiveness are patterns commonly used as a defense against the discrepancies between how parents and children view themselves and others' expectations.

As overachieving parents, we primarily use communication to instruct our kids, unearth information, and reprimand. This is a limited use of communication. When family members know how to express their thoughts and feelings clearly and willingly, a bond develops. This use of communication is the best way to build trust and respect among family members.

Effective communication is composed of two elements: attentive listening and open, nonjudgmental response. When you identify and use the skills involved, your interactions will support the exchange of thoughts and feelings so that family members feel accepted and understood.

When we parents were growing up, two-way communication was a rare occurrence in the family. Often our parents' approach was: "Don't talk back to me!" This oft-repeated warning prevented any real communication by telling us loud and clear that our thoughts and feelings were irrelevant. Most of us talked back anyway, enraged at the powerlessness we felt at being denied the opportunity to give our point of view.

Now that we're dealing with our own children, it is useful to remember how that rage felt, how it filled our ears with heat and hurt us inside, making it impossible for us to hear what our parents were really trying to tell us. Perhaps if we remember our own childhood experiences clearly, we will refrain from shouting the same unhelpful directives at our children when we don't know what else to say. After all, implied in the "Don't talk back" rule are other damaging messages:

- "You're supposed to do what I say without question."

- "I'm in charge."

- "I know what is best for you. You're just a kid."

Authoritarian behaviors produce underachieving attitudes in children. As a parent, it is critical that you rethink how you communicate. You cannot rely on the role models provided by your own parents because experience has shown that those communication patterns were ineffective.

Unlocking the Door to Effective Communication

Changing the patterns of communication between you and your child is a matter of trust. As the parent, you are responsible for creating a climate in which trust can thrive. Your child needs to know with absolute certainty that you will listen; be responsible for owning your thoughts, feelings, expectations, and actions;

respond openly; and be willing to see her point of view in order to resolve your differences.

I have taught the guidelines for effective communication hundreds of times during parenting workshops and to families in therapy. These practical, easily understood techniques have improved underachieving behaviors and family relationships. There are seven guidelines in all. The four designed to improve your ability to listen are:

- Show your readiness to listen.
- Listen attentively.
- Defuse emotional triggers to understand feelings.
- Keep track of facts, logic, and reasoning.

The three that improve your ability to respond are:

- Identify and express your emotions.
- Restate what was said.
- Use questions to help your child sort out the problem.

Guidelines for Effective Communication

Listening Skill #1: *Show your readiness to listen.* In order to communicate with your child, you need to listen attentively and then respond thoughtfully. This process requires your total attention. For example, it's important to avoid a serious conversation when you've just walked in from a long day at the office or are rushing to fix dinner. You must be sensitive to your child's moods and teach him to be sensitive to yours. The simple question, "Can I talk to you now?" helps to clarify the other's readiness to listen. When you want to talk, ask your child if he is prepared to listen and teach him to do the same with you. Effective communication takes place only when both people are emotionally available.

Simply arranging for an appropriate discussion time will avert many misunderstandings and hurt feelings. One of my clients, Tracy, explained how failing to do so got her and her daughter Joan into a painful situation. Joan came running into the house one late autumn day excited about finally getting a B on an algebra midterm. When Tracy grunted and didn't give Joan the response she felt her achievement deserved, Joan said sarcastically, "Don't get too excited! No matter what I do, it isn't good enough for you!" She then stormed into her room and slammed the door.

Tracy was already upset. She had just gotten off the phone with her ex-husband and was disturbed by one of their continual arguments about child support. His refusal to contribute financially to the family put enormous pressure on her to increase her sales production in a new, highly competitive job. When Joan slammed the door, it felt like the last straw to Tracy. She went up to "talk" to Joan and the fight was on.

Joan knew that her mom had been rooting for her on the test; Tracy had said so right before Joan left for school. But it hurt her feelings when her mom didn't respond to her news about the good grade. Had Tracy been able to tell Joan that she was upset at the moment but wanted to hear all about the test in a few minutes, the whole episode could have been avoided. And had Joan been accustomed to requesting, instead of demanding, her mother's attention, she might have felt less disappointed.

It is important for both of you to observe and become aware of each other's moods before demanding or expecting attention. This sensitivity to the other is part of being respectful. When you need to discuss something with your child, always ask first if she is in the frame of mind to hear you. If your child says no, set a later time to have the discussion. You are not asking your child's permission to have the discussion; you are simply arranging a mutually agreeable time.

If you are unavailable emotionally when your child wants to talk to you, it is your responsibility to say, "I would like to listen to you, but right now is not a good time because I have other things on my mind. How about tonight after dinner?" Setting up a specific time when you or your child can listen is a way of saying, "I respect your right to be who you are."

In order for your children to communicate easily, they need to feel safe. If you are upset, tell them why you can't listen and let them know that your mood has nothing to do with your feelings toward them. This prevents them from thinking they are the cause of your unhappiness, a conclusion underachievers automatically draw. It also models for them a self-aware behavior that they can imitate to improve their own communication at home and elsewhere.

It's easy to forget the impact we have on our kids, especially when we have something serious on our minds. One of my clients, Betsy, described to me how one evening she was going through the motions of straightening up the family room when her thoughts were on her job. Her division at work was being reorganized, and the possibility of being laid off from her prestigious job was causing her paralyzing anxiety. She didn't hear her 11-year-old son, John, come bouncing down the stairs calling her name. John was relieved that he had finally finished cleaning his room and looked forward to going out to play. But sensing his mom's bad mood, he tensed up automatically, assuming she was angry with him. His immediate thought was, "What did I do wrong now?" He felt a tightening in the pit of his stomach and tried to make himself invisible, but that meant he couldn't ask her if he could go out to play.

I taught Betsy (who later taught her children) to announce her moods to the family by making simple statements like, "I'm having a rough day, but I'm not upset with you." Over time, Betsy's new approach helped John to relax. He no longer judged himself as harshly as he had been doing.

Just the simple awareness of availability to listen will make a big difference in family dynamics. Six months after I finished working with the Stevenson family, Mrs. Stevenson called to give me some updates. Whereas once both children had been at risk for academic and discipline problems at home and at school, now they were on the honor roll and both participated in extracurricular activities. Moreover, they were happy. I said to Mrs. Stevenson, "Tell me, which skill had helped the family the most?"

Without hesitation, she responded, "Listening to each other." The Stevensons were now so committed to effective communication, they rearranged their living room and removed the television to make it more conducive to intimate conversation. All family members knew that when they went into the living room, it was time to give each other their total attention and respect.

Listening Readiness Check

1. Before you begin a discussion, ask the person you want to approach, "Is this a good time for you to listen?"

2. If not, set up a specific day and time and be prepared to give each other your undivided attention.

3. Arrange to meet in a pleasant environment, without interruptions.

4. Inform family members if you are preoccupied or in a bad mood and therefore unavailable. In such instances, be sure to set a time later to talk.

Listening Skill #2: *Listen attentively.* "You never listen to me!" shouted Deanna, 16, in a therapy session with her mom, Kate.

"That's ridiculous, I always listen to you!" her mom fired back defensively.

"Whenever I'm talking, you're doing something else."

"Well, I'm still listening, aren't I?" countered Kate.

"That's not really listening!"

Another client, Terri, told me, "My mom makes up her mind before I even finish what I'm saying and then won't listen to my point of view. I hate her for that! She doesn't care about what I say!"

Kenneth hated it when his father asked him why a chore wasn't done. Before he could get out two words of explanation, his dad launched into a tirade. And when Wanda wanted to share with her mom her excitement about getting her first A on a composition, she was dissuaded when her mother continued folding the laundry. In fact, she interrupted Wanda's excitement to say, "Take these up to your room."

Deanna, Terri, Kenneth, and Wanda all felt discounted. Chances are your child does too. Indeed, the most frequent complaint I hear from underachieving children is that their parents don't listen to them. By learning to listen attentively, you can heal this emotional wound and make your child feel important and accepted.

Listening is the most important but the hardest aspect of communication for parents. Telling your child what to do is such a large part of parenting that listening may feel like a threat. Subconsciously or consciously you may fear you are losing control. But listening to the information your child is willing to volunteer sends her the powerful message that you are interested in what she has to say. Every time you listen and respond, you are telling her that you value her accomplishments, thoughts, and feelings. This acknowledgment builds a child's self-esteem. When children receive the undivided attention of a parent, they feel loved; when they don't, they feel rejected.

For your child to feel loved, however, such listening must be unconditional. Now, that's a tough order for many parents. Unconditional listening means you have no ulterior motivate; you are willing to listen without judging or manipulating the information given you. Most of us are accustomed to ferreting out information as we listen and then using that information to control or "parent" our kids.

Kathy, a busy real estate agent and mother, was concerned with her 16-year-old, Bill, because he was dating one steady girl—a first for him. As Kathy was fixing sandwiches for the family, Bill came into the kitchen to grab a soft drink. Seeing that he was in a good mood and approachable, Kathy questioned him about his relationship with his girlfriend. Her queries appeared to Bill as sincere interest. But as soon as Bill said, "Amy and I are making plans to go to college together," Kathy interrupted.

"Your puppy love isn't likely to last. It's silly to count on being together when college starts. You should decide where you want to go without considering Amy's choices so you don't end up in a college that's wrong for you."

Predictably, Bill did not want a reality check at that moment. From the way Kathy was maintaining eye contact as Bill talked, he thought his mother sincerely wanted to hear about his girlfriend, but when she interrupted with her opinion, he was sorry he had opened his mouth, particularly since Kathy had used the information he revealed against him. All he wanted from his mom was for her to listen—nothing more. Feeling betrayed and manipulated, he stormed out of the room, silently vowing never to reveal to his mother anything personal again.

Kathy made the mistake of listening with a hidden agenda. She wanted to find out what was going on in her son's life. If parents want to establish trust, they should not make the mistake of appearing to be listening when they are really trying to catch their kids doing something wrong or expose some character or behavior flaw. When parents pounce on such a "flaw," give their opinion, and then prevent their child from carrying out his plans, he feels seduced, manipulated, betrayed, and angry. He will become increasingly guarded in what he subsequently shares. Think of it this way: Would you continue to volunteer information to someone who repeatedly responds with criticism, suggests another way, or makes some unwanted and unappreciated comment or rule? Children want you to accept them for what they think and feel. Listening can give this feeling of acceptance only if it is unconditional.

In my experience, many parents fear that if they listen attentively to their children, they will convey the impression that they agree with the youngsters when in fact they don't. What I tell my clients is that *listening and agreeing are quite distinct.* Listening is allowing your child to fully express her thoughts and feelings about a certain topic. Agreeing or disagreeing only comes after you have heard what she has said. Then, you make a decision by taking into account what you heard. Your child may still become upset with your decision, but because of your willingness to listen, she won't accuse you of not caring about her. Disagreements don't have to be associated with anger and fighting. Once you and your child become comfortable with effective communication skills, you will be able to listen respectfully but still parent judiciously.

Adam Thompson, a successful lawyer, was confronted by his son, Peter, for never taking the time to listen when the boy asked for privileges. During a therapy session, Adam admitted that he cut off his son because he felt at a disadvantage when Peter presented one of his "airtight" cases. It seemed to Adam that if he listened to one of his son's requests, he would have to defend himself for his parental decisions. "It is just easier," he said, "to break in and get angry when I hear something I disapprove of. That way he knows he won't get his way."

Of course, Adam's interruptions made Peter feel discounted. He believed that Adam's parenting decisions were arbitrary and negative because his dad didn't love or like him. During a therapy session, Adam agreed to listen to Peter without interrupting to discover his own emotional response.

The following week Adam came to the session angry. He gave an example of what happened when he didn't interrupt.

Peter wanted to go on a ski weekend with his friends. This was the first time Peter had initiated such a trip. He had been on other ski weekends originated by adults. He had arranged every detail so his parents would know the who, why, when, where, and how of it. Peter figured that when his dad heard the trip was logically set up, complete with chaperon, getting permission would be just a formality. He didn't consider the possibility that his father might disagree with his participating in such an activity in the first place. When Peter finished his presentation he expected an answer.

Adam felt as if he had to mobilize all his thoughts, evaluate the plan, and decide how to respond on the spot. He was unsure of his position about the skiing, because he had not encountered this situation before. Yet he felt pressured to respond quickly in order to appear sure of himself in front of his son. He thought decisiveness would prevent Peter from manipulating him. So despite his ambivalence, he quickly denied Peter's appeal. Peter became furious and accused his dad of not really listening.

During our session, the Thompsons developed some listening rules (listed below) with the conscious realization that listening and agreeing are distinct activities. Either Adam or Peter could ask for time to think over a decision before responding.

Attentiveness Check for Parents

1. Are you ready to give your child your undivided attention?

2. Are you prepared to maintain eye contact with her?

3. Are you willing to provide enough time to allow your child to finish what she has to say?

4. Have you remembered that listening and agreeing are distinct activities?

5. Are you prepared to take your time before responding?

Listening Skill #3: *Defuse emotional triggers to understand feelings.* We communicate to convey information and feelings. Often we don't take the time to label our emotions, but we express them through the words we chose and the intensity with which we say them. When we don't tell others how we feel, we leave it to them to interpret our emotional state. They may or may not be correct. Unspoken emotional states inevitably cause reactions in us as we listen. We can all feel another's anger even if he doesn't say, "I'm angry!"

If you are unsure of why or with whom your child is angry, it is easy to believe that the emotion is directed at you. Conversely, if your underachieving child doesn't know the cause of your being upset, he automatically thinks, "Now what did I do wrong?" As a result, he may become defensive or withdrawn. As parents, we can easily be drawn into reacting to our child's emotional state rather than listening to what he is saying. Consequently, our response is based on our emotional reaction instead of the facts of the situation.

When I first started working with Carl, age 17, and his parents, he and his dad, Tom, were engaged in constant emotional fights. When Carl was 10 years old, he had announced that he wanted to become a veterinarian. Tom couldn't have been happier, and he used Carl's new interest to motivate his son to get better grades. Even though Carl did well, his marks still weren't as high as his dad wanted them to be. Tom kept reminding his son that he needed to do better if he was going to be a vet.

By the time Carl reached the age of 16, he knew he had been wrong about his career choice. He tried to tell his dad that his plans had changed so he could drop out of advanced biology class (which he hated), but Tom just yelled at him, forbidding him to do it. Carl dropped the class anyway. When the school sent home a copy of the class change, Tom was livid. Father and son came into a therapy session fuming. After 10 minutes of listening to them yell at each other, I intervened and asked if anything had been resolved.

Both became silent because they recognized they were just repeating themselves. I asked father and son to write down their feelings about each other and the situation. That would help them to let go of some of the anger. Then I had them sit opposite each other so they could make direct eye contact. I instructed Tom to listen to all of Carl's spoken and unspoken feelings to fully understand his son's position. This was not the time for Tom to respond. He needed to keep his emotions in check by paying attention to what Carl was saying.

Carl talked for 10 minutes without stopping. I then asked Tom to tell us what he had heard and felt of Carl's feelings. For the first time, Tom realized the depth of his son's anger and frustration. Carl was angry because his dad usually didn't listen or seem to care about what he thought or felt. He felt frustrated because he feared his dad might be right—he couldn't make good grades. As Tom listened to the intensity of Carl's self-doubts and observed the angry clenching of his son's fists, he was devastated.

"I understand now how you feel, son. Why didn't I listen before?" he said sadly. "I thought that I was trying to motivate you and that you didn't care. I had no idea I was undermining you."

I asked Tom what prevented him from listening to his son before. After reflecting on the situation, he said, "Carl's anger about the situation felt like a personal attack. I guess I got really defensive. I turned my attention to what I was going to say to defend myself and my opinions." Tom had gotten caught in reacting to Carl's feelings instead of listening to them. Carl, at the same time, was using his anger to get his dad to pay attention to him for once.

Reacting to your child's feelings instead of simply listening to them triggers unnecessarily hurtful interactions. When your child is expressing his feelings verbally, it is your job to remain objective in order to learn what he has to say. To do so, remind yourself that your child has a right to his emotions and that you have a choice to react or to remain objective. Deep breathing might help keep you calm. By gaining some distance from your youngster's emotions, you'll be in a much better position to understand what the situation really means to him. Listening to the way a statement is made will help you understand the intensity of the problem.

When your child has finished expressing himself, it's important for you to tell him what you heard his feelings to be. If you're unsure, don't be afraid to ask how he is feeling. Your query supports your child in better understanding himself. For example, Tom reflected back to Carl the feelings that he heard in a simple statement: "Carl, I hear you're angry and frustrated."

Often youngsters don't take the time to think out their feelings before expressing them. They are just starting to recognize their emotions as they relate to you. When you reflect back what you have heard, you help them become more aware of their feelings. They can then clarify what is important to them in the situation. Moreover, by reflecting what you heard your child say, you avoid misunderstandings. You might want to ask, "Did I understand you correctly?" at the end of your reflecting statement. You might also inquire, "Are there any other feelings you want to add?" When your child sees that you support his right to his emotions, this validates him as a unique and special person.

Checking the Feeling Message

1. Stay objective and remember it is your child's feelings that are being expressed, not yours.

2. Your job is to listen to your youngster's feelings, not to react to them.

3. Identify the feelings he expresses through words, tone, and nonverbal cues.

4. Reflect back to your child the feelings you observe with simple statements such as, "I hear you're angry and frustrated."

5. Ask if you heard correctly.

6. After reflecting what you heard to your child, ask if there are any other feelings he would like to add.

7. Ask him what he is feeling if you are unsure of what you heard.

Listening Skill #4: *Keep track of facts, logic, and reasoning.* Now that you know how to keep emotions from interfering with your attentive listening, you need to discover the reasons behind your child's emotions. Children draw conclusions based on their needs. They have a difficult time putting their needs aside to be objective about a situation or even to remember the facts. By listening for your child's emotions and then listening for the reasons behind her emotions, you will help your child separate fact from fiction and avoid interpreting situations in ways that make her feel criticized and unloved.

Facts are statements that can be proved by using our five senses or by consulting an established authority for verification. But no matter how valid the facts, each person's application of logic and the reasoning process is unique. Starting with the same facts, you and your child may not reach the same conclusion.

Greg and Matt experienced a simple situation of coming to different conclusions when Greg gave his son a new sports watch. Greg recognized that Matt had been putting a great deal of time into his homework recently. His grades had improved significantly since the last report card. Greg wanted to reward Matt for his effort, hence the present. Matt, on the other hand, concluded that maybe the unusual gesture meant that his father *did* love him after all. Father and son drew different conclusions about the gift: to Greg it was a reward for effort, to Matt it was a gift of love. Because of his perception, Matt expected more presents from his father as a continuing sign of being loved. That set him up for disappointment. To Greg, the present was a "one-shot deal" to encourage his son.

It is important to observe how your youngster reasons things out, how she lines up the facts, so that you understand the route she takes to arrive at her conclusion. As you listen to your youngster, you'll need to separate the facts from her conclusions. Remember, it is her story you are trying to understand.

To see just how easily children lose sight of the facts, consider the reaction of Frances, age 9, to her mother's inability to come to her school's Valentine's Day play. When Bev came home late from her floral shop that evening, Frances wouldn't speak to her. Finally, Bev went to her daughter's bedroom and asked in an exhausted tone, "What's the matter, honey?"

"Your job is more important than me! You even like your flowers better than me!" Frances said angrily. "You were the only mom that wasn't at the Valentine's Day play! You don't love me!" she wailed. Instead of becoming defensive, Bev took her child in her arms and said, "I see how hurt you are that I didn't go to the play. I hear you say that you think because I was so busy today, I didn't care about seeing it. Is that what you think?"

When Frances nodded yes, Bev reminded her that the problem was that the play fell on Valentine's Day. "Remember when we talked about the fact that Valentine's Day was going to be busy for me so that I couldn't come to your play?" Frances nodded again. "I also heard you say that my absence meant my business is more important to me than you. I love you and feel so badly that I couldn't come. But I have the time now to hear all about the play."

Because Frances felt hurt, it was easy for her to forget that she and her mom had talked about Bev's absence. Also lost for Frances was the fact that for a florist, Valentine's Day is one of the most important days of the year. Bev encouraged Frances to look at the facts again and draw a different conclusion, one that helped Frances recognize that her mother really did love her.

From this example, you can see how children draw conclusions based on their needs and can have a difficult time putting those needs aside to be objective or to remember the facts.

Underachieving children draw conclusions that support their belief that they are unlovable and defective. That is why it is imperative to reflect to your child the facts. Also probe to get all the information. Restating the facts your child used to reach her conclusion helps you understand her reasoning, lets her know you've heard her, and clarifies the situation for both of you.

Checking for Understanding

1. Listen for the facts, logic, and reasoning your child used to draw conclusions.

2. Ask questions to elicit the facts if they aren't immediately apparent.

3. Reflect to your child the facts you heard and ask if you heard them correctly.

4. Check your child's reasoning by saying, "Because of this (state the fact), you thought that (state the conclusion)."

5. Restate the facts if your child has used faulty reasoning.

Responding Openly and Nonjudgmentally

Listening provides you with all the information you'll need to understand how your child is thinking and feeling. You now have the opportunity to respond openly and nonjudgmentally. This is the second stage in the communication process that supports underachieving children.

Being open means you are willing to share your feelings and thoughts with your child. Being nonjudgmental means that you will not evaluate your child as wrong, stupid, or defective because of what he says. Rather you will work with the information he provides and respect his point of view. For example, if your youngster feels that he can't do anything right, don't dismiss his statement as ridiculous. Instead, recognize it as his perception of the problem. To solve the problem, accept that what your youngster has to say is the truth for him. By acknowledging your child's feelings and thoughts and the conclusions he draws about himself, you validate his perception of his life experiences. This encourages him to be open and communicative with you. If you discount, deny, or dismiss his thoughts and feelings, he will shut down. If you are judgmental toward him, he will lie.

Your child's trust in you grows only if you consistently respond to him openly and nonjudgmentally. When he can trust you to refrain from attacking him because of what he reveals, honesty develops and trust deepens. And an honest, trusting relationship is necessary if your child is to change his behavior.

Joey was working hard to use the test-taking skills he had just learned. He thought he had done well on his social studies test because he followed all the steps that had been outlined in a therapy session. When he got a D on the test, he didn't know whether he could tell his parents the truth. He was afraid they would be terribly disappointed in him, especially since he felt they were now treating him well. "Maybe they'll start telling me I'm lazy, like they used to before I came to therapy," Joey fretted. But as he wrestled with this problem Joey started thinking about the changes in his relationship with his parents. They listened to him now, and that made him feel good about himself. Indeed, he felt more comfortable in being honest with them. As soon as he reviewed the changes in his family he knew he would have to tell his parents the truth, even though it might be hard and scary.

When Joey showed his dad the test, Martin said, "I see how disappointed you are, and I too am disappointed that the study method didn't work for you. But let's go over the test and find out what went wrong. How does that sound to you?" Joey was so relieved that his father didn't yell or call him names, he started to cry. Martin put his arms around his son and said, "There is nothing that we can't work out together."

Martin preserved his son's dignity by focusing on the situation and how Joey felt about it instead of judging the boy. This dad was also able to consider the situation objectively without becoming emotionally involved. Martin made it clear that he was disappointed, but he was able to recognize that the issue was about Joey and not about his parenting skills.

It's important for you to refrain from criticizing or controlling your child or hiding an agenda when you respond to his communications. Below are three guidelines for responding openly and nonjudgmentally.

Responding Skill #1: *Identify and express your emotions and thoughts.* During your lives together, you will have many opportunities to be angry with your child. How you express your anger can make the difference between hurting her or helping her see the consequences of her behavior. As an adult, you have the responsibility to express anger in a controlled way. If you are upset and have not taken the time to think through the situation (to discover what is causing your anger), you are prone to acting irrationally. Only when you can identify the cause of your anger and are clear about what you want to do about it will you be ready to express your feeling to your child.

The most appropriate way to communicate your feeling is to make "I" statements that express what you are feeling and what is causing you to feel that way. With "I" statements you own your emotions, without blaming your child for them. After all, your youngster didn't cause your anger. Your reaction to his behavior is the basis for your feelings. And you can choose how to react.

Examples of "I" statements include:

- "I get frustrated when I have to remind you to do your chores."

- "I feel unappreciated when I see your new clothes on the floor."

- "I'm furious that you lied to me."

- "I resent the tone of voice you are using."

- "When you ask me to pick you up at school, and I have to wait for you, I'm irritated."

Larry saw how destructive reacting emotionally can be. Brian, age 11, had agreed to water the lawn every Wednesday as part of his weekly chores. When Larry came home from work on a Wednesday evening he noticed that the lawn was dry and casually reminded his son of his commitment. Later that evening, right before the boy's bedtime, Larry asked again about the watering. Brian went outside and turned on the sprinklers. They were supposed to stay on for 15 minutes. He got ready for bed in the meantime. Unfortunately, he forgot about the sprinklers and fell asleep. Larry didn't discover that they were still on until he locked up the house for the night, two hours later.

The next morning, Larry jumped down Brian's throat. "I can't believe how stupid you are! You couldn't even remember to turn off the water last night," he shouted. "Now the new seed will be ruined and it's your fault. It was bad enough that I had to remind you twice to put the sprinklers on in the first place. Where the hell is your head? If the lawn is ruined you are not only going to pay for it, but you'll replant it, too. You disgust me, get out of my sight!"

Brian was devastated and, understandably, went to school crying. Larry had labeled him stupid, irresponsible, and incompetent. Underachievers are all too used to hearing these messages. If parents make such judgments, kids feel they must be true. To make matters worse, Brian was already feeling guilty and disappointed in himself when he discovered his lapse. So now, not only did his father judge him as inadequate but he also criticized himself. His father's outburst further diminished Brian's self-esteem and resolved nothing. Unfortunately, this show of anger was not a guarantee that the boy would remember the next time to do the watering without being told.

As Larry and I reviewed the incident during a therapy session, we worked on how he could have responded differently to Brian, still letting his son know about his anger but without the inappropriate character assassination. Larry came up with the "I" statement, "I'm angry with you because you didn't follow through with your responsibility of watering the lawn. Since the water was left on so long, you and I need to see if there was any damage and decide what we are going to do about it." If Larry had said this instead of launching into a tirade, Brian would have clearly seen that his dad was angry about his carelessness and expected him to take responsibility for it, but he would not have felt attacked.

By being judgmental, you automatically cut off any communication with your child. Consequently, you prevent the situation from becoming a learning opportunity and you fail to resolve the problem. You will be left angry and so will your child. When responding to your youngster, state how you are feeling and explain why. Staying with the facts of the situation will help you focus on what actually happened instead of seeing things through your anger. Emotions can easily cloud reality.

Check for Expressing Your Thoughts and Feelings

1. Identify your feelings and thoughts before making a statement.

2. Express how you are feeling and state what caused the feeling.

3. Start the statement with "I."

4. Use the format: "I feel (state how you feel) because (state the reasons you feel that way)."

Response Skill #2: Restate what was said. Another way to respond nonjudgmentally is to restate your child's feelings and thoughts without giving your opinion or perspective. Your goal is to respond to the situation from your child's point of view. Restating statements take the following form:

• "I understand how disappointed you are because you didn't get the grade you felt you deserved."

- "I hear that you are angry because you feel your curfew time is too early."
- "I see how frustrated you are because I didn't let you invite your friend to sleep over tonight."

Maria, who had been very popular in school, was always reminding her 14-year-old, Rosa, that to have friends one had to look pretty and get good grades. Rosa, however, had a negative self-image. She believed that she could never do well in school and she saw herself as unattractive. Consequently, she was depressed and insecure much of the time. Eating was Rosa's only escape from depression.

Maria would approach Rosa whenever she saw her daughter was feeling down. She hoped to get her to talk. But every time Rosa started expressing her feelings, Maria jumped in with, "If you would only go on a diet and stick to it, everything would be all right." This further depressed Rosa. Not only did she hate herself for being overweight, but she felt guilty that she couldn't stick to a diet.

As we worked in therapy, Maria realized that her "helpful" reminders about dieting were, in truth, hurtful statements that contributed to Rosa's anxiety. Eventually, she realized that she couldn't force Rosa to lose weight or to get good grades no matter how many ways she tried to motivate her. Instead, she learned to restate Rosa's feelings.

For example, Rosa complained about clothes shopping. "I hate my body," she said heatedly. "I know the clothes I like won't look good on me." Maria was now able to restate Rosa's sentiments nonjudgmentally: "I see how frustrated you are about shopping. You are afraid that if you find something you like, it won't fit you."

Since Maria wasn't campaigning for Rosa to diet, the pressure was off Rosa to defend herself and she was able to talk about how embarrassed she felt about her girth. When Rosa came to her mother a week later and said, "I want to lose weight," Maria listened attentively and then asked, "What can I do to help you?" This approach worked. Over time Rosa started losing weight and became more interested in all her activities. She even improved her grades.

Without your criticism, your child is able to stay clear about her issues and not get tangled in an emotional reaction to your point of view.

Check for Restating What You Understood

1. Identify your own agenda and set it aside.

2. Listen to what your child thinks and feels about a given situation.

3. Restate what you hear your child saying. A simple "I hear you saying..." will do the trick.

Response Skill #3: Use questions to help your child sort out the problem. Even if you know what needs to be done in a situation, you won't help your child by dictating to her what to do. That only brings resistance and resentment. Underachieving children feel controlled by authoritarian parents and fight their suggestions—and rightfully so. After all, the solution you come up with may fail to take into account your child's perception of the situation. By forcing her to adopt your point of view, you're asking her to discount her own.

Asking questions that are not emotionally charged or judgmental is a useful technique for helping your child arrive at her own course of action. In so doing you encourage her to become objective so she can take responsibility for the situation.

Debbie, 16, had a difficult time dealing with her parents' divorce. She alternated between anger and depression. To make matters worse, she and her mother, Joyce, had to move from their expensive home to a condominium in a different city to be near Joyce's new job as a bank manager. Debbie expressed her feelings of powerlessness in rebellious, self-destructive behavior that distressed Joyce. Often Debbie would stay out past her curfew and she defiantly talked back to her mother. Joyce tried to tell her daughter what she needed to do to adjust, but each suggestion was met with anger and resentment. The relationship between mother and daughter quickly deteriorated. They came to therapy.

As we worked together, Debbie became better able to accept her situation and get on with her life goals. She finally brought home a B average. She and her dad had agreed that when she got B's, he would buy her a new car. After driving it for only three weeks, however, she rear-ended another car and did major damage to both. Even though witnesses said the car in front stopped suddenly, Debbie was cited by the police, and her insurance company had to pay. The teenager was beside herself. She didn't know how to tell her father, with whom she had difficulty communicating. The millions of questions he would ask would make Debbie feel attacked. That might cause her to become even more emotional, the very reaction her dad hated. She came to Joyce in distress, dreading that her father would take away her car.

Joyce was sympathetic because she anticipated her ex-husband's reaction. But even though she knew how Debbie could handle the situation, she thought it wise not to interfere. So she proceeded to use questions to help Debbie sort the problem out.

"How do you feel about yourself, Debbie?" Joyce asked.

"I'm disappointed in myself," Debbie explained. "I'm scared, too. Now I realize that driving is a serious responsibility."

"Well, Deb, I can see how disappointed you are with yourself because of this accident. What are you going to do about it?"

"I don't know. I'm so confused," cried Debbie.

In the course of their conversation, Joyce asked Debbie a myriad of questions:

• "How are you going to tell Dad?"
• "How do you think Dad will react?"
• "What might be the best time and place to talk to him?"

- "How much can you offer to pay toward the insurance deductible and the increase in the insurance premium?"
- "Do you think it's important to let your dad know how you are feeling about this?"
- "Do you have a plan to present to him if he threatens to take away the car?"

Instead of making suggestions that would cause Debbie to rebel, Joyce helped her daughter face her responsibility for the accident and its aftermath, regardless of whose fault it was. By asking questions nonjudgmentally, Joyce presented Debbie with all the variables she would encounter when she talked to her dad. In the process of answering her mom's questions, Debbie identified and expressed her feelings, evaluated the facts of the situation, and came up with a plan of action.

Using this questioning approach, you can support your child in dealing effectively with her problems. Questions beginning with the words "How," "When," "Where," and "What" help your child clarify her thinking and broaden her perspective. But the word "Why" will stop conversation because it implies that your child has the problem figured out. The only response you get when you ask "Why?" is the famous chant, "I don't know."

Check for Supporting Through Questioning

1. Have you set aside your idea of how your child should handle the situation?

2. Have you armed yourself with questions that start with "How," "When," "Where," and "What"?

3. Are you prepared to ask questions that address all the factors involved in the situation?

The Natural Rhythm of Listening and Responding

During a conversation with your child, you move naturally and easily between listening and responding. But these two processes may or may not be used together. It is important to recognize when a response is or is not required. That comes with practice.

After your child is finished talking, pause for a few seconds before you respond. This allows her to add any forgotten thoughts and gives her time to ponder her experience. This also gives you time to figure out how you intend to respond. If you want to give a solution, first ask yourself whether your child requested one. If not, don't offer one. If her statement was unclear, then restating what you heard may prompt her to add additional clarifying information. If you think you did not hear all of her thoughts or feelings clearly, ask about the missing information. The point is to support your child to share her thoughts and feelings comfortably. When in doubt, ask her if she wants to share more about the situation.

Yvonne came home from school in a quiet state, an unusual demeanor for her. "You look unhappy, Yvonne. Would you like to talk about it?" her mom, Sheila, asked calmly.

Between sobs Sheila discovered that Yvonne didn't get the part she wanted (or any other part) in the class play. Sheila listened patiently until Yvonne was completely finished. "This must be disappointing for you. How are you feeling about it?" she inquired as she put her arm around Yvonne.

"It makes me sad and a little angry at the teacher because I thought she liked me," Yvonne answered.

"Do you think the teacher picked the student she liked best for the part?" Sheila asked.

Yvonne hesitated for a moment and then said, "Karen did a good job when she tried out." Sheila waited. Since Yvonne said no more, she went on to another subject.

Later that evening Sheila asked, "Are you all right, Yvonne?"

"You know, Mom," the girl grinned, "next time I'm going to practice before the tryouts like Karen did."

"That's a good idea, Yvonne," Sheila replied. Sheila didn't

force the issue with her daughter but just responded to what she was able to understand about the situation.

By being open and nonjudgmental, Sheila helped Yvonne draw her own conclusions and resolve the problem at her own pace. Had Sheila become angry with the teacher or had she agreed that the teacher was unfair, Yvonne would have missed an opportunity to get in touch with what the situation meant to her.

As the skills presented in this chapter become a part of your daily interactions with your child, both of you will appreciate the changes they produce. Your youngster will recognize that he can escape old self-defeating patterns. And you will gain confidence and reassurance that you can help your child to outgrow his underachieving behaviors.

Chapter Eight

Supporting Your Child in Getting Where He Wants to Go

N ow that you are comfortable with effective communication, you can begin helping your child identify and accomplish his goals. When you complete this chapter and put its principles into action, you will help your youngster learn how to set and reach goals. Since school is such a large part of a child's life, I will be focusing on how to achieve school goals, but the techniques presented work for all goals. From this chapter, you will gain a clear understanding of good study habits and other skills your child will need to polish in order to improve his grades. Your youngster will have a much better sense of how to schedule homework and free time. And you will have an accountability system to cut through excuses and help him stay focused on his goals.

You can use the lists of suggested guidelines in this chapter (especially those applicable to helping your child improve school performance) as a script. In fact, I encourage you to work directly with your child from these guidelines.

Whenever I have used this material as a teacher, school counselor, or therapist, parents as well as children have expressed an immediate sense of hope. They understand that their difficult situations are going to change for the better. The guidelines clearly state parents' and children's roles in the process of achievement. Both now have new and discrete job descriptions!

The best way to help your child achieve is to teach her how to get things done. Being overwhelmed causes kids to procrastinate or balk at a required task. Your youngster needs a systematic approach to an assignment, no matter how large or small. She must identify the steps and skills needed to complete it. As an achieving adult, you probably do this automatically, but it's worthwhile to think about what techniques you've perfected to ensure your success. Reflecting on how you handle work projects and resolve problems may provide insight into the importance of developing systems that fit your individual style.

Underachieving children lack similar systems because they are often trapped in immobilizing negative thoughts and feelings. Helping your child create a plan of action and listening to and supporting her in her feelings and thoughts will enable her to change her behavior.

Each child works differently, so be ready for your youngster's input. Her approach may be different from yours, but that's okay. Don't let your agenda get in the way of listening to her. Remember that you are helping her develop a system for herself. If she's to adhere to the new system, she needs to know she was a part of creating it.

Helping Your Child Make Sure a Goal Is Right for Him

If your youngster decides to accomplish a task that you believe is worthwhile, you may be delighted and may want to help him.

But often when he expresses a desire, it is just that—a desire—not a carefully laid-out plan. You may have one vision of what he is talking about but he may have another. If you do not communicate your perceptions of the goal, problems can arise as you try to help.

Your youngster reveals his interest, commitment, and motivation through the communication process. Those are the issues that you need to work with. The actual goal that your child chooses is secondary for now. Your role first is to teach him the strategies he'll need to achieve *any* goal. If you try to influence his goal, you may find yourself in a power struggle (see chapter 9). On the other hand, once your child sees that he can achieve what he has set out to do, the quality of his new goals will correlate with his greater level of confidence.

Gerry's parents brought this sixth-grader to my office. Stu, an engineer, complained that his son was doing passably well but didn't "go the extra mile." When I asked for an example, Stu said, "When Gerry signed up to earn eight merit badges in Boy Scouts, I had to police him to make sure the work got done. I've told Gerry he can't wait until the last minute because there is too much to do. I'm tired of worrying about how we will get everything done."

As Gerry listened, he clenched his fist and tightened his jaw. When I asked about his unspoken anger, he said, "I wanted to earn the eight badges, but Dad is making too big a deal about it. It doesn't all have to be perfect the way he says. He keeps telling me to redo stuff because it's not good enough. I wish he would just stay out of it!"

"Who decided you should earn the eight merit badges?" I asked. Both father and son claimed the other had made the decision, which signaled to me that the topic had never been completely discussed.

As we worked together, we discovered that the badges had a different significance for Gerry than for his dad. Stu thought the badges should represent the very best Gerry could do, so he would be proud of wearing them. According to this dad, earning eight merit badges meant a big-time commitment. He assumed Gerry had the same attitude, and he was willing to help his son. Gerry, on the other hand, just wanted to complete the eight badges required to advance to the next level of scouting. He felt neither the necessity for his dad's help, nor any particular pride in earning the badges.

Since father and son had never discussed these issues, it was easy to see how their problem arose. Gerry and Stu had unspoken and contradictory expectations about how the other was to behave. They were each working toward different levels of proficiency. Gerry and Stu applied themselves to the goal without specifying what it entailed or what each one would do. Stu needed to be aware of his assumptions regarding the "right way" to earn merit badges. Gerry needed to think about why he wanted the badges at all, and if he was willing to spend a good deal of time on acquiring them. Had Stu and Gerry discussed the goal more fully, they would have recognized the disparity in their expectations for the outcome.

Below are some helpful questions parents and children can use to clarify the goal under consideration and the child's motivation toward reaching it.

Questions to Ask Your Child About His Choice of a Goal:

1. Why would you like to do this?

2. Is this something you really want to do or something that you think might be just fun to try?

3. How much time are you willing to spend on this?

4. What will it take for you to be satisfied that you've accomplished the goal?

5. Is this your goal or do you feel someone else is influencing or pressuring you?

Questions to Ask Yourself:

1. Whose idea was this goal?
2. Why do I think my child should pursue it?
3. Did I influence my child in any way?
4. What level of proficiency do I think he should achieve?

Breaking Down the Task and Checking for Competency

Even if you and your youngster decide on a common goal, you still need to clarify the level of proficiency each of you expects. Creating a standard of proficiency is difficult for the under-achiever because of his past failures and present self-defeating attitudes. Kids are naturally full of ideas and want to explore many new avenues. But the underachiever's natural desire and enthusiasm quickly wane when he runs into an obstacle, no matter how small. Obstacles include tasks that are too difficult, and those that take more time or require more skills than antici-pated. An underachiever doesn't have the experience to trust his abilities or judgment. So before he establishes a specific goal and decides the proficiency level to work toward, he first must break down the task into its component parts to check whether he has the required competency.

Underachievers are easily overwhelmed by their own and others' goals. When they can't immediately figure out a natural sequence to accomplish a task, they become confused, embar-rassed, and angry.

Dick wanted to teach his 12-year-old, Kevin, to be more responsible. Dick felt that Kevin was doing poorly in school because he had never had any household responsibilities. Dick believed that was why Kevin was too undisciplined to do his schoolwork.

When Dick told Kevin that he would be responsible for mowing the lawn henceforth, Kevin complained that it would take him all day and he wouldn't have time to go skateboarding with his friends. Despite his protests, he tackled the job, but the task seemed too big and difficult to Kevin. The lawn never looked perfect because he couldn't get the mower close enough to the flower beds to trim the grass neatly. Consequently, even after a herculean effort, Kevin never felt pride in his yard work. Besides, his father always found something wrong with it.

After many fights, Kevin and Dick made a list of the specific tasks the job entailed: mowing the grass, trimming the edges and flower beds, and sweeping the sidewalks. Then they assessed Kevin's skill level at each task. Dick realized that he hadn't taught Kevin the tricky maneuvers necessary to get the mower near the flower beds. One by one, Dick approached each flower bed and lawn area, demonstrating the skills needed. Each maneuver became a small goal for Kevin to accomplish.

The following few weeks showed a marked improvement in Kevin's yard work and his attitude toward it. Dick made a point of asking Kevin how he felt the job was going, often pitching in and helping to check and reinforce his son's developing skills. With Dick showing cooperation and concern, Kevin felt valued. This eliminated his feeling that his father was simply ordering him to do something that he didn't want to do himself.

Offering to help your child learn a new skill, encouraging him in accomplishing that goal, and showing appreciation for what he has done provide strong motivation. The process also creates meaningful contexts for you and your youngster to get to know and appreciate each other. When the situation is under your control, as with household chores, it is relatively easy to the break down skills, check for competency, teach the necessary skills, and encourage your child. However, your child must also achieve goals in other arenas, such as school, sports activities, and music or dance lessons. Even though you may not have control over your child while she participates in these activities, you may still be concerned about her performance and want to help her do her best.

It is especially difficult to help your child improve in school. You share the authority for your youngster's learning with her teachers and the school. Since you don't have direct knowledge of how your child is doing in the classroom, it is difficult to know precisely what to do. Furthermore, each year teachers, grading standards, texts, and classroom rules change. Effective communication skills become even more important because you'll be depending on your child's point of view to break down the necessary skills and check for competency.

Kevin and Dick's successful lawn-mowing experience gave father and son the confidence to tackle the seemingly more difficult task of improving Kevin's grades. As we began the session I recognized Kevin's inherent desire to do well. All children have a natural need to learn, but it is often arrested when they feel bad about themselves.

Kids, even underachievers, are usually aware of their classmates' grades because at some level, they comprehend that knowledge is power in our society. I asked Kevin, "Who gets the A's in your class?" He rattled off the names of several of his classmates. I then asked, "How do these students get the A's?"

"That's easy," he replied. "They participate in class, ask questions, do all their homework, and study for tests."

I pressed him to be more specific about the skills necessary to get good grades. Also I asked him questions to assess the competency level necessary at his grade for each skill. In this way we would know exactly what skills he needed to learn in order to be a successful student. Reproduced below is the list of skills and questions that I used to elicit information from Kevin.

It is difficult for underachievers to break down tasks, but by exploring these questions with your child, you demonstrate the steps necessary to achieve good grades. Your youngster will have the opportunity to think about the skills he already has, which can boost his confidence. He'll also discover which skills need further development.

Classroom Skills

To be a good student, you must...

1. Participate in classroom discussions.

   - Do you raise your hand or wait until the teacher calls on you?
   - How do you feel when you answer a question and the teacher says it's wrong? How do you handle it?
   - Can you recognize that being wrong is a natural part of the learning process?

2. Ask questions.

   - Do you feel comfortable asking questions in class?
   - Do you worry about what your classmates will think?
   - Do you worry about embarrassing yourself?
   - Can you keep in mind that asking a question shows your desire to understand?

3. Take complete notes when the teacher lectures.

   - How do you take notes?
   - Do you copy and star everything the teacher puts on the board? This information will usually show up on tests.
   - Let's look at some notes you have taken recently. If they are incomplete, what can you do to make them more complete?

4. Write down all assignments.

   - Do you have an assignment book?
   - When do you write down assignments?
   - How often do you forget to write them down?

- Do you have the telephone number of two reliable friends in each of your classes so you can call them if you are unsure of an assignment or forgot to write it down?

5. Make sure you understand your homework assignment.

- Do you look at the homework assignment before leaving the classroom?
- Do you ask for clarification if necessary?

6. Listen to the teacher when he or she is lecturing.

- How long can you pay attention to the teacher without thinking about something else?
- Do you find yourself daydreaming in class?
- When is it easy for you to pay attention?
- When is it difficult?
- Can you think of questions about the topic and then listen for the answer?

7. Teach yourself to concentrate on "boring" or difficult material.

- What can you do to refocus yourself on what the teacher is saying?
- Can you pretend that it is the most interesting thing you have ever heard? That way, you'll become absorbed enough that the material will make a mental impression on you.

8. Cover absences.

- Here again, it is important to have the telephone numbers of two reliable friends in each of your classes so you can call them to ask about assignments during your absence.
- Do you feel okay calling these friends when you are absent and asking them to please take legible notes so you can copy them the next day?
- Who can help you with homework if you missed the explanation of an assignment?

Homework Skills

To be a good student, you must...

1. Complete all homework.

   - Who can you ask for help if you need it? Can you ask your teacher for help? Is there a classmate you can get help from? Can you ask a family member? Do you need a tutor?

2. Hand in homework on time.

   - What gets in the way of your doing your homework?

   - What do you find yourself doing when you are supposed to be working on homework?

   - How might you reorganize your time or allow for breaks to make sure you complete your homework?

3. Pace long-term assignments by breaking down the task into shorter weekly segments.

   - Do you like to work for long periods of time?

   - Do you like to work for shorter periods of time but more often?

   - Do you like to do a weekly assignment all at once, or would it be easier for you to break it up and do some every night for, say, three nights a week?

As Kevin answered the questions, we learned that he didn't have a system for writing down his assignments. That caused him to "forget" to do his homework. He never used his book bag because it was such a mess, and half the time he couldn't find it in the morning anyway. Because he didn't have a designated place to keep his classroom notes, he often lost them. All this helped explain why his test grades were poor. Kevin simply didn't have all the information he needed when he had to study for a test.

It became clear that Kevin's inability to organize his materials and daily routine accounted for many of his school problems. Dick helped Kevin develop an evening routine for getting his clothes and assignments ready for the next day. They decided that when Kevin finished an assignment, he would put it in a new notebook under a section labeled "homework." He would then put his notebook in his book pack and review each assignment sheet to determine if he needed to bring anything else to school the following day. Once his books were organized in the book bag, he'd place it next to the front door. In the morning all he had to do was get up, shower, get dressed, eat breakfast, and grab the bag, with full confidence that he was prepared for his day at school.

A formerly tense situation transformed to a smooth, 45-minute routine. Whereas Kevin used to leave the house every morning in a bad mood, now he sailed out the door eager to greet the day. By being better organized, Kevin felt more secure and confident as a student. Your child can, too.

Who's Responsible: Defining Your and Your Child's Roles

Helping your child learn specific skills may sound easy. Indeed, teaching the skills of yard work, household chores, family responsibilities (such as baby-sitting), and resolving sibling disputes are well within most parents' competency. For the most part, once you pinpoint the skills, break down tasks into manageable units, provide the needed instruction in an encouraging context, and agree upon a mutually acceptable division of labor, things usually work themselves out. It is difficult, however, to move from the role of parent to that of teacher and then back again. As parents, we have a vested interest in seeing that our children succeed. This can create a strained teaching situation. Nowhere does the tension become more apparent than in the area of homework. When you are trying to help your child with homework, not only must you remember long-buried information, but you must also approach the material as the teacher does today—no easy task.

Jason, age 16, was having a difficult time in school. His dad, Fred, a well-known district attorney, became furious whenever he thought about his son doing so poorly. Fred decided that he was going to make sure Jason got good grades. When he came home each night, Fred expected Jason to be ready with his book, paper, and pencil to get the homework done in short order. Tired and irritable from a long day at work, Fred became impatient when Jason didn't understand how to do the things he explained. "I don't understand why you can't get it!" he'd say, or "I just told you how to do it. Weren't you paying attention while I was talking?" or "What's the matter with you?" You're just not trying hard enough!" Jason claimed that some of his dad's comments made him nervous and unable to concentrate.

Unconsciously, Fred expected to explain each task only once, and he expected Jason to catch on quickly and do the assignment correctly. He didn't realize that he wasn't explaining the task in a way that Jason could understand, or in the same way his teacher had presented it. Whenever Jason interrupted with questions, Fred explained again, using the identical words. Rather than help Jason, this approach rendered him even more frustrated and inadequate. And, because Fred couldn't make Jason understand, he too started feeling frustrated and inadequate about his teaching skills.

To compound the problem, Fred's vow to make sure Jason got good grades caused him to become even more emotionally invested in the outcome. Finally, Fred felt the sacrifices he was making by giving up his limited free time just weren't paying off. His tension escalated whenever he started doing homework with his son. Anything Jason did set him off. Jason, meanwhile, hated to work with his father. He became even more aware of his dad's anger than of the information he was trying to convey. Here again was a situation in which expectations had not been clarified and realistic goals not set.

Fred and Jason needed to decide who was responsible for what. During a therapy session, they set goals for the next grading period. Jason's goal was to get in all of his homework and classroom assignments on time. Next, Fred and Jason went through the list of the tasks necessary for Jason to complete his work on time. Fred discovered that Jason didn't know how to take class and textbook notes or how to study for tests. Now he understood what was holding back his son. The family decided that Jason would ask his teacher how to take class notes and then request to see his friend's notes after school, to make sure he was getting all the important information. Also, Jason enrolled in a note-taking class given through the local community college. Fred would teach Jason how to study for tests, since he had been a straight A student and knew many effective preparation techniques.

During therapy, Fred realized that his guilt over Jason's grades was linked to his guilt over spending too little time at home. These feelings made it difficult for him to establish appropriate boundaries for his responsibilities. When he overreacted and set aside too much time for Jason, he became tense, frustrated, and easily angered. He wasn't taking enough time for himself.

Jason sensed his father's mood and misinterpreted it as anger directed toward him. In response, he shut down. Jason also saw how much his dad wanted him to get good grades. But he felt that the goal of better grades really belonged to his dad, not to himself, so he gave up. That was easier than actually exploring his capabilities.

During therapy, Fred acknowledged that he was willing to help when requested. He instructed Jason to call him at his office by 4:00 P.M. if he would need help that night. In that way, Fred could arrange his schedule to make sure he was at home and emotionally ready for Jason.

Your child needs to have a procedure for asking for help. This supports him in thinking about the areas in which he needs help and gives you the opportunity to adjust your busy schedule and be emotionally and mentally available. But keep in mind that daily parental help is a sure sign that your youngster isn't taking responsibility for himself, and that you are too invested in his grades.

Go back to the task list and determine which skills your youngster lacks. If he is following the tasks necessary for being a good student, he should need only occasional help. If a specific subject is particularly difficult for him, hire a tutor so that he can learn the missing skills. Don't try to be a tutor yourself.

When I helped Jason and his family define their responsibilities, we wrote down the decisions so everyone was clear about the agreement. Below are some questions that will help ensure that your family responsibility checklist encompasses all the important information.

Who's-Responsible-for-What Checklist

1. What skills does your child need to learn?
2. Who is going to teach them to her?
3. How long will the lessons last?
4. When and where will the lessons take place?
5. When and how are you going to evaluate whether your child has learned the skills?
6. What are you responsible for?
7. What is your child responsible for?

Being Realistic

Helping your youngster set realistic goals means that he:

• knows what he wants to do

• understands the tasks and skills involved in reaching the goal

• knows where to get help if necessary

• correctly estimates the time required to reach the goal

Underachieving children have difficulty estimating how long it will take them to do tasks. They lack the life experience that teaches them their competencies. Consequently they have trouble managing time.

Robbie was a bright teenager who had had good grades until his freshman year in high school. As his grades dropped, his parents became angry and alarmed. Robbie was depressed and felt he had let himself and his parents down. He wanted to do well, but somehow he couldn't make himself finish his homework. Indeed, as time went on, he stopped doing it altogether.

After Robbie began therapy he recognized that his attitude toward homework was not supporting the grades he said he wanted. "I don't think it's fair that I have to do so much homework," he rationalized. "The school system is all screwed up. If the teachers can't teach us what we need to know during class time, then it's their fault. Why should I have to waste all my time doing busy work?"

This adolescent hadn't adapted to the change in work load from junior high to high school. In junior high, he was assigned little homework and earned grades good enough to satisfy himself and his parents. He felt high school should be the same and resented the change.

During therapy, Robbie was able to look under his anger and uncover deep feelings of inadequacy. He had been underestimating the time necessary to complete his assignments because he really didn't want to face doing them. When he did attempt the work, there never seemed to be enough time, so he would rush through and do a sloppy job. After we made a list of the tasks and skills needed and checked for competency, we were ready to look at how this youngster managed his time.

I asked Robbie to log his daily activities for a week to help him see how he spent his time. He discovered that he wasted a lot of time by listening to music before starting his homework.

The music usually led to other spontaneous activities, and before he knew it, it was too late for him to do his work. By tracking how he spent his time for a week, Robbie clearly understood how his choices prevented him from achieving his goals. In therapy he learned that if he scheduled a finite period for homework and made a calendar for the week, he was able to participate in sports, hang out with his friends, and still do well in school.

Underachieving children resent the time they spend doing homework because the activity makes them feel inadequate. All their self-doubts are activated. Since most underachievers don't recognize these feelings, they start looking for external reasons to explain why they hate doing homework. The natural excuse is that homework takes up too much time; it will prevent them from doing what they want or having any time to themselves. Kids resist finding out the truth about how they spend their time because once they do, they can no longer use this rationalization. Underachieving kids don't want to give up their excuses. If they do, they will have to face the real issues.

Nevertheless, addressing how your kids spend their time is essential if they are to reach their goals. Helping youngsters create a concrete plan lets them put their goals into action.

You might make a weekly calendar and ask your child to fill in how she spends each hour. As you review the calendar with her at the end of the week, tally the hours and put them into categories such as:

- school and religious instruction
- household responsibilities
- extracurricular activities
- sleep
- sports or special interests
- playtime (or for older kids, time with friends, either in person or on the phone)

- TV
- computer games
- time alone
- maintenance (dressing, eating, bathing)

Then re-sort the totals under two new categories: mandatory and optional activities. In this way, you can help your child evaluate how she's using her time and what she's getting from her activities. If there are differences of opinion about what is optional or mandatory that seem to be turning into power struggles, chapter 9 will give you some helpful pointers.

Scheduling Homework and Free Time

A schedule analysis will help you show your youngster that it's possible to find time for having fun, playing sports, and doing homework. Use the following guide to help your child identify how time can best be used.

1. *Ask your youngster to observe how she is currently using her time.* Make a log as suggested above. Help your child account for each hour in the week. If she cannot, list the unaccounted hours in the "free" or "optional" category. She will be amazed how much time "escapes" her.

2. *Help your child learn to estimate the time for school assignments.* Suggest that she time herself when she does homework for different subjects. This will give her a more accurate picture of how long her assignments should take. Underestimating how long homework or school projects take is a major cause of poor performance. If your youngster underestimates, she is likely to become restless, to rush through the assignment, to leave it incomplete, or to abandon the next assignment. It is easier if your youngster mentally prepares for a longer study

period. If she completes her work earlier than estimated, she'll enjoy her extra free time.

3. *Encourage your youngster to take advantage of weekends.* Many students feel the weekend is totally "their" time so they often lose the advantage of working on long-term projects or studying for a test. However, because of the long stretch of unstructured time, the weekend is ideal for homework or study. Putting in 2 or 3 hours of work on Saturday and/or Sunday on a regular basis can help your child keep his grade point average high without interfering with his pursuit of enjoyable activities. After all, if he puts in 3 hours on Saturday, he'll still have 21 hours left to do what he wants. It will also relieve him of undue pressure during the week.

4. *Ask your child to list favorite activities and what he derives from them.* For example, after your son has studied for a test, he might want to shift to an activity that doesn't require concentration, such as riding a bike, talking on the phone, or visiting a friend. Taking a break from studying by visiting a friend is appropriate but spending five hours at the friend's house far exceeds the need for a break. (Your child probably can get the relief he needs and say everything he has to in a much shorter time, saving longer visits for another occasion.) He may find that he also needs to expend energy in a physical activity after doing homework. Or, to prevent frustration, he may want to relax by reading a good book before tackling his math assignment. As he becomes more self-aware, your youngster will observe how certain activities affect his emotional state. He'll be able to plan for the activities that give him energy and pleasure. He will prioritize this list of activities with ease.

5. *Help your child plan her activities in advance.* Having it all—good grades and an active social life—is often a matter of a student's learning to schedule her time in advance. With a plan, she can focus clearly on what she wants to accomplish at the moment without the fear of losing out on an activity she values but hasn't planned for. Suggest that she either buy or make a

calendar to carry with her or hang on the wall of her room. Show her how to pencil in her homework assignments (especially long-term projects), obligations, sports practice, afterschool events, and recreational activities for the week.

Encourage your youngster to appreciate that her activities can fit into the week without the loss of free time. This helps her see that her goals can be achieved. She will no longer feel stressed or overwhelmed.

Accountability Systems: Choices and Consequences

As children go through the steps to achieve their goals, many activities such as TV, computer games, friends, phone calls, and eating can easily sidetrack them. To help your kids stay focused, you'll need to develop an accountability system. An accountability system incorporates goals, required tasks, division of labor, and consequences for failing to follow through. In short, it clearly defines who is responsible for what and what will happen if your child doesn't follow through.

Underachieving children have highly developed excuse-making and manipulation mechanisms. It can take a great deal of time and effort to break through their defensive posture to arrive at the truth of any situation. But an accountability system can cut through underachievers' excuses.

Patti wanted to try out for cheerleading at the end of her freshman year. When she mentioned it to her parents, they said they would sign the permission slip if she agreed to improve her grades. At first, Patti thought it unfair that her parents were making her get higher grades than the school required. Grades were a continuing battle in the family. Patti's mom, Renee, was a well-known oceanographer and her father, Ted, was the president of a large company. Both had competitive jobs to which they felt dedicated. They were disappointed that their daughter cared more about her social life than her schoolwork. Even though Patti tried to get her parents to change their minds about her grades improving, they held firm.

After reviewing the skills necessary to get good grades and checking for competency, Patti used a tutor to catch up on missing skills. Now, she needed to take responsibility for doing her homework and studying for tests. During a therapy session, we set up a homework accountability system that stated the time she would finish her homework, where she would put it for her parents to check for completion, and the consequences if she failed to comply.

When developing such a system, be sure to take into account your child's homework style. Some students like to go straight home, get a bite to eat, get their homework out of the way, and then talk on the phone or watch TV. Others work best after a break from sitting down all day. They may begin homework after dinner.

Forcing your child to ignore her style will create resistance to the task before she begins. If your youngster is unsure about which approach works best, try a week of each. Patti found she worked most efficiently when she hit the books as soon as she got home from school.

Decide when it is reasonable to have all homework ready to be checked. For elementary grades the deadline might be 6:00 P.M.; for middle-school students, 8:00 P.M.; and for high school students like Patti, 9:00 P.M. or later. By establishing a daily deadline, you'll never have to ask "Do you have any homework?" or "Why aren't you doing your homework?" or even become tense about checking up on your child. The established deadline will be the first time you become involved with the issue.

Also, decide together the best place to put the completed work. An assignment sheet should accompany the homework. This lists all the homework and tests given in class, thereby letting you know what has to be done.

It is the child's responsibility to do all of her homework every night by the agreed-upon time and to leave it in the designated place. If these procedures are not followed, you must step in, since by her actions your child is saying, "I am choosing not to be responsible for myself today." If the homework is not completed by the designated time (and not a minute later), instruct your child to go to her room immediately and finish her work. At that time you should also impose the predetermined consequence, such as loss of TV, phone, computer, or social privileges.

Whatever consequence you choose, it should remain in effect for no longer than 24 hours. For example, when Patti did not complete her homework by 9:00 P.M. Monday as agreed, her parents instructed her to get off the phone immediately to do it. They also reminded her to bring her phone to their bedroom, as she would be barred from using it or any other phone until 9:00 P.M. the following day.

Making the consequences effective for a 24-hour period prevents kids from giving up or developing an "I don't care" attitude that can result from long-term consequences (such as no phone privileges for two months). The purpose of establishing consequences is to teach cause and effect. When your child does her work, there are privileges. When she doesn't, there are consequences.

Ideally, your youngster will write down all assignments, complete homework on time, and improve her grades. However, the fact that she requires a homework system in the first place implies that she doesn't quite grasp that good grades cause a person to feel good about herself, gain knowledge, and make both you and her happy.

It is essential, then, to discuss with her the role trust plays in the homework accountability system. Obviously, you can only check those assignments that are listed on the sheet. Therefore, it is important to tell your child that you will be calling her teacher to find out if there are any missing assignments after the system has been put into effect for several weeks. Say this naturally so she recognizes that she will be held accountable for her behavior. Also, statements such as, "I hope you will chose to do your homework every day. If you are having any problems with it, I will be glad to help you," show your child that homework is her responsibility.

If, however, you find there are missing assignments, you need to face the fact that your youngster has chosen to be dishonest. Since dishonesty is highly destructive to any family, a serious consequence for this behavior needs to be established in advance so the child knows what to expect. Patti's consequence for missing assignments was a five-hour work detail. This can be very effective, especially if the work begins on Saturday at 7:00 A.M. or earlier. (Adjust the number of hours for the work detail if your child is younger than nine.) Be specific about what you expect your youngster to accomplish on such a work detail. Examples of jobs that are good for this type of work detail are: cleaning the grout between tiles, washing windows, sweeping out the garage, weeding the garden, and washing the dog. Make your standards clear and review the procedures for doing the job. Don't allow your youngster to do anything else until she has finished her work detail and you've checked it. Believe it or not, your child may feel a certain sense of satisfaction when she completes the job. But please don't expect her to thank you for this opportunity.

It is wise to check with teachers after the first two weeks of implementing a homework accountability system. You can make phone contact or ask your child to present each teacher with a letter asking if she has missed any assignments during the last two weeks. Ask the teachers to sign any messages they write to you. Most will happily cooperate since they will have noted an improvement in the work handed in. Depending on the results, you may or may not have to make regular contact with your child's teachers. Additionally, when your youngster's report card comes, look for any indication of missing assignments. If there are any, then previously established consequences should go into effect automatically.

It is important to stick to the rules and be consistent. Children will test boundaries, even those they help set. If your youngsters see that you are unswayed by excuses and bursts of emotionality, they won't use these ploys to wiggle out of their responsibilities. Besides, the consequence will prevent them from participating in favorite activities.

When systems are well thought out and written down, there is no need to lecture your child about inappropriate behavior. Everyone knows what is expected and what will happen if the rules are broken. Your job is to follow through with the consequences if your child fails to do what was agreed upon. Your child is responsible for following through with his commitments, which means doing the work or receiving the consequences. An accountability system prevents any surprises—and surprises are a breeding ground for arguments. Homework, like any other goal, is no longer an uncharged battleground. It is clearly mapped territory.

Chapter Nine

Turning Power Struggles into Teamwork

A power struggle is a contest of wills between two people with distinctly different points of view. Each person wants to win. You may be trying to get your child to do homework or household chores without being asked or fighting about it all the time, but he has a mind of his own. On the other hand, your child may want you to stop nagging about responsibilities, but you're unwilling to let go.

By the intensity of the interaction during a power struggle, you become more aware of your unconscious expectations for your child and your child becomes aware of his demands on you. You are focused on what you want and how you feel. Power struggles are intense because you are both fighting to maintain your position, fighting as if your very survival is at stake. Once you lose the upper hand, you believe your adversary (in this case, your child) has defeated you. Not wanting to feel powerless, you hang on at all costs.

Powerlessness can trigger many self-doubts within parent and child alike:

- "Can I stand up for myself?"
- "What if I'm wrong and my child (or parent) is really right?"
- "Do I truly believe what I'm saying or am I reacting to feeling controlled?"
- "I have to get my way to prove I'm my own person (or to prove that I'm in charge), don't I?"

Even if you and your child are unaware of these thoughts, they influence your words and actions.

During power struggles you and your child may find yourselves overreacting, making overgeneralized, emotional statements that you don't really mean.

As a parent you might say:

- "You're grounded for the rest of the year!"
- "You can never leave this house again!"
- "You are going to practice that piano for five hours every day!"

Your child might say:

- "You're mean!"
- "I hate you!"
- "I wish I had a mother like Susan's."

In this chapter, you will learn an eight-step program to prevent power struggles. These steps are:

1. Recognize the price you pay for power struggles.
2. Separate your agenda from your child's.
3. Evaluate how your past influences today's decisions.
4. Become objective about your child.
5. Develop a joint vision of who your child is.
6. Establish and reinforce house rules.
7. Agree on privileges.
8. Use teamwork to resolve differences of opinions.

Let's explore these steps in greater depth.

What Price Are You Willing to Pay to Win?

Achieving parents truly feel they know what's best for their children. They think, "If only Caroline would go for the gold medal/get an A in math/run for class president, she will see the light and become the achieving child I know she can be." From the parents' point of view, there is a right and a wrong way to approach tasks. The right way, according to overachieving parents, is for their child to adopt their way!

Christmas was a special time for Fran. This year her eight-year-old, Beth, was mature enough to help bake the cookies to be given to friends and family. Fran wanted to make this a mother-daughter tradition, so she included Beth in the shopping and planning. Both were excited. They enjoyed themselves as Beth helped Fran mix the dough and cut the cookies. But when it came to the decorating, a power struggle ensued.

Fran wanted the gingerbread men decorated her way because she had gotten many compliments in previous years. Also, she wanted them to be especially beautiful, now that she could tell everyone Beth had helped decorate them. But the eight-year-old had her own ideas. She didn't understand why the gingerbread men should have only three buttons. "Why can't they have mustaches or pink eyes?" she asked.

Every time Fran corrected her daughter, Beth said no to her mom's suggestions and continued doing it her way. Finally Fran said, "Beth, this is the way you have to decorate the cookies if you want to help Mommy. If you can't do it this way then you can't help me at all!"

Beth was devastated. She left the kitchen crying and refused to eat any of the treats at Christmas.

The cookies did look beautiful that year. But was the power struggle worth it? Unfortunately, Fran's need to have "perfect" cookies made her critical of her daughter's innocent attempt at creativity. It also interfered with the very goal Fran wanted to achieve—a close relationship with her daughter.

When Fran brought up this issue in therapy, she was distressed about what had happened. "Why did I make this such a big deal?" she wondered. "I didn't realize I was being so critical until Beth started crying!"

I asked Fran, "Can you remember when you felt criticized as a little girl?"

After a few minutes, she said, "Whenever I wanted to do things my way, my mother would tell me it was wrong and that people would reject me if I did it like I wanted to."

When I asked how she felt when her mom said those things, Fran replied, "I remember feeling scared and frightened that I didn't know the right way. I felt as if I had to do things perfectly so no one would reject me."

Fran's unresolved childhood pain influenced how she parented her own daughter. She wanted Beth to do things perfectly, too, so that she also wouldn't be rejected. Now Fran realized that she could have given Beth her own cookies to decorate and suggested that she share them with whomever she wanted—her friends or her family.

Who's Making the Agenda for Your Child's Life?

Power struggles bring out unresolved childhood issues within us. These issues can impinge upon our relationships with our kids, as in Fran's situation. We may be unaware that we need to have our own way in order to feel safe or in control. This need causes us to campaign for our own agenda without taking into account our child's point of view. Unfortunately, our lack of self-awareness can affect our self-image and our parenting.

If you stop to think about the motivation behind your own achieving behaviors, you might be able to see how your childhood affected your values.

Russell, 48, was encountering difficulties convincing Brad, age 12, to value getting outstanding grades, excelling at a sport, appearing neat and tidy at all times, being organized, and respecting his elders. Brad wanted to wear his hair long and didn't care if his room looked "lived-in." Furthermore, he saw no need to pressure himself into getting straight A's. Life was too short. Besides, he was planning to attend the local junior college because it offered the music program he wanted.

The power struggles between father and son escalated. Russell became more dictatorial and rigid while Brad became more oppositional. Brad's mother, Allison, fed up listening to them complain about each other, made the appointment for father and son to see me.

After listening to their anger, I asked Russell, "What's so important about Brad following your formula for success?" Russell looked shocked. To him the answer was obvious. He said, "That's how you get people to pay attention to you."

Then I asked, "When did your parents give you attention as a little boy?"

"Whenever I said something my dad thought was intelligent, he would respond. But he ignored me if he thought I said something stupid," he replied.

So I said, "Russell, I'd like you to think back. Pretend you're a little boy of nine and tell me what it's like to be ignored."

To Brad's amazement, Russell started crying. He shared the pain of feeling rejected and inadequate. Then he admitted, "I wanted my son to learn everything in school so he would never feel stupid, put down, or ignored." A bit embarrassed by his show of emotion, he added, "I didn't think that childhood stuff still affected me."

After I explained the power of the subconscious and its ability to influence our thoughts, feelings, and behavior even if we're no longer aware of specific incidents, both Russell and Brad were eager to talk about childhood memories.

It's important to remember difficult incidents as well as your emotional reaction to them. Once Russell understood the origin of this need to be perfect, he was able to respond thoughtfully to his son, without the overlay of old childhood issues. Father and son were able to openly discuss Brad's desire to work with synthesizing music. Since the power struggle no longer dominated their lives, they both benefited from their talk. Russell understood his son's aspirations, and Brad had a more realistic picture of his future career options. Based on their conversation, Brad recognized the benefits of a four-year college; it would add variety and depth to his store of knowledge.

If you find yourself doggedly holding a point of view and fighting for it without hearing your child's perspective, then most likely some of your childhood issues have been activated in the fray. These unresolved issues repeatedly trigger ancient emotional reactions. Getting in touch with your painful memories allows you to reexperience the original feelings. But now, as an adult, you can decide if your habitual reactions support you and your parenting or cause problems in your life. If you have ongoing conflicts with your children, you can be sure that unresolved childhood issues are contributing to the difficulty. As a child those painful experiences may have left you feeling powerless and helpless, but as an adult you have many more resources to help you deal with them.

The exercises in the following section will help you evaluate your options and resources so that you no longer have to react automatically when your youngster hits one of your emotional buttons.

How Your Personal Issues Influence Your Parenting

The business of life keeps us so active and involved with immediate needs that we may forget to stop and evaluate our emotional lives. Habitual behavior can prevent us from staying attuned to our changing thoughts and feelings. In order to short-circuit power struggles, it's important to spend some time reflecting on who we have become and where we are going. This reflection helps us recognize how our life experiences, especially those in childhood, influence parenting.

In the following exercises, Part I helps you explore your emotional state right now. Part II deals with your childhood—the inner child within you. These questions are designed to stir up feelings and get you thinking, so it's best to answer only a few at a time. You may want to start a journal and use your answers as jumping-off points for further self-exploration. Allow yourself to expand upon your answers by writing down specific incidents. Remember, the point of this exercise is to help you become aware of the motivations behind your interactions with your kids.

Part I: Thinking of the Present

1. What areas of your life bring you joy?

2. Does your adult life match your childhood fantasies of it? Have you had pleasant surprises? Have you had disappointments?

If you feel life has let you down, it is easy to want to protect your children from similar disappointments. That reaction may be inappropriate, however, because your disappointments relate to your failure to meet your expectations and hopes, not your child's. Ask yourself whether you are trying to prevent your child from failing as a compensation for your own disappointments and failures.

3. Do you know how to make yourself happy? Have others' demands overlaid your vision of yourself so it's difficult to be in touch with your true self?

It's important to distinguish the values you have developed through your life experience from those that others try to get you to adopt. This question is designed to help you become aware of whose agenda you are living: yours, your parents', or your significant other's?

4. What should you change in your life so that you can more readily express your true self?

If you have recognized that you react to the expectations of others, then you may need to reevaluate your activities. To do so, ask yourself whether an activity drains your energy and deflates your mood or enlivens you and elevates your mood. If it's draining, chances are you're fulfilling someone else's expectation.

5. Evaluate your parenting experience. What are some of the joys? What are some of the disappointments?

As we grow up, we imagine what it will be like to be adults and have families. Our personal fantasies combine with our parents' modeling to form our perception of parenting. But as we experience life, our preconceived notions may not materialize as planned. As you evaluate what parenting means to you, pay attention to whether you are still using your fantasy as a criterion. Use your answers to clarify your own parenting standards.

6. What are some of your current strengths and weaknesses that you hadn't allowed yourself to recognize earlier?

Look at yourself objectively and nonjudgmentally. Ernie, a 42-year-old lawyer, saw that his quick temper damaged his relationship with his son. Once he admitted this, he was able to rechannel his anger constructively.

7. What do you think and feel about yourself now?

Cheri, 38 and mother of one, knew she was a competent, successful freelance journalist but she still suffered anxiety and insecurity on a regular basis. Her thoughts about herself reflected a positive self-image but her feelings reflected low self-esteem. This disparity put her at war with herself and undermined her clarity in parenting. If you see a discrepancy between how you think about yourself and how you feel, it is time to examine where the negative thoughts and feelings come from. Part II will help you.

Part II: Thinking of the Past—Childhood and Adolescence

Use the following questions as guidelines to help you get in touch with your feelings and thoughts about the major developmental stages of your life:

- preschool years (birth to five years)

- elementary school years

- junior high school years

- high school years

- college years

Compare your answers for each developmental phase to help you understand how you have evolved into who you are today. Also observe how thoughts and feelings from the past influence your adult perceptions and your approach to parenting. Connecting your past life experiences to your present parenting practices is a vital link to becoming objective about your child. Allow the following questions to ignite the memories of your childhood experiences.

1. What made you happy? What was important to you?

2. Of what and whom were you afraid?

3. How and when did you get attention from your parents, teachers, or other authority figures?

4. How did you get along with others your age? Were you a bully or did you get bullied? Were you shy or popular? Did your friends listen to you? Were you a leader or follower?

5. Describe your relationship with your parents. Do you feel you were a disappointment to them or were they proud of you? What do you think about your parents as individuals?

It is often difficult for adults to reexperience the hurt or anger they felt as children toward their parents. Many feel guilty for having those negative emotions. Others (like Brad's father, Russell) dismiss them, thinking that the pain happened so long ago it couldn't possibly affect them today. The point, however, is not to judge or blame your parents for your emotional pain. For the most part, they did the best they could. Rather, this exercise should help you become aware of your feelings.

6. What and who hurt you emotionally or made you feel bad about yourself? How did that happen?

You can be hurt by the people you trust. Think back on these people and review how they treated you.

7. What did you want from your mother and father that you didn't get?

You may want to write them a letter pretending to be a certain age. (To recall early school years, for example, you might want to print using your less dominant hand. This will help re-create how you felt at that time.) Get in touch with your feelings, then decide whether or not you wish to share them with your parents.

8. Whom did you want to please? Whom did you want to emulate? Who were your heroes?

The people you want to please and be like have values you admire. The heroes you picked can help you recognize the traits you valued during different periods of your life. Identify what you admired about those heroes and explore whether you have incorporated those values into your life.

9. What were some of your favorite books, movies, songs, TV programs?

From this information, you will see what and who influenced you.

This list is just a beginning of your self-exploration and discovery, so allow your feelings and thoughts to be your guide. After reviewing this self-exploration, you are ready to observe your relationship with your child and to understand how to be objective with her.

How to Be Objective About Your Child

Overachieving parents often see their children as extensions of themselves. Unfortunately, this causes clashes of wills, for in truth, children are not extensions of their parents. They are unique and separate individuals.

Your need to define yourself as a person or parent can cause you to see your youngster through the filter of who you think she should be. But consider the damage to your child: If you don't support her individual strengthens and talents, she will doubt herself. That can lead to a negative self-image; feelings of rejection, helplessness, and powerlessness; and the fear that she will never fit into life. These negative feelings and thoughts cause underachieving behaviors.

Barry, a 20-year-old sophomore at an Ivy League school, came into counseling because his parents were concerned about his desire to change majors. Barry knew he didn't want to stay with pre-med studies, but he had no idea what he did want to do. Throughout school, Barry had shown real aptitude in art classes. When he talked about majoring in art in college, however, his father, Mitchell, took him on one of their many evening walks to explain the facts of life as he saw them. Mitchell calmly listed all of the flaws in Barry's plan and then added the logical reasons why his own perception would work.

Barry was caught in a bind. While he respected his father—a successful businessman and former Green Beret—he always felt bad about himself after these walks. Often he would say to himself, "How could I have been so stupid to think my idea would work? Being a doctor would be more secure and worthwhile to humanity than being a commercial artist. Since Dad is so successful, he must know what's right!"

Unfortunately, Mitchell wasn't being objective about his son. He was still dealing with unresolved issues from his own past. Barry's grandfather had been a well-respected physician. Mitchell was known as "Doc's son." While Mitchell wanted to be a doctor too, he was afraid that he would never live up to his father's standards. He left home early and went into business. Mitchell's father was a cold, stern man who only acknowledged his son when he excelled. Mitchell never felt loved by his father, so consequently he didn't know how to express love toward his son. This dad thought that love meant making sure Barry was successful, and what career could be more prestigious than medicine? Because Barry also felt that the only time his dad loved him was when he excelled, he had been trying to please his father his whole life.

After Mitchell worked out his relationship with his father in individual therapy, he was able to observe his relationship with his son. Soon, he became more objective about Barry. For the first time, he recognized how depressed Barry became after their walks. He also saw how creative his son was and how intensely he felt about world issues. Father and son started to discover each other. Mitchell asked Barry's opinion on world events. He discovered his son's preferences in movies, TV programs, food, and clothes. Instead of trying to force Barry into a mold, he began to help him learn who he was.

At first, it was difficult for Barry to make his wishes and desires known. This was the first time his father had allowed him to have his own opinions and make decisions based on them. But as Barry recognized that his father wouldn't criticize him, he felt safer to express himself.

To become objective about your child, observe your relationship with him first. Then seek out his preferences, likes, dislikes, and opinions. Invest time to learn who he really is. Regard your child not as part of you but as an individual who happens to be related to you.

Below are guidelines to help you apply your self-discovery to the task of becoming more objective about your child. This activity will help you to develop a joint vision of who your child is becoming so you can support the magnificence within him!

Becoming Objective About Your Relationship with Your Child

You learn a great deal about yourself when you observe your interactions with your child. Many of the traits that bother you about her are characteristics you also dislike in yourself. Moreover, what you enjoy about her tells you something about yourself.

You have a different relationship with each of your children, so repeat this exercise for each child.

1. Observe your child's strengths and talents. Be specific. What does she do well? What comes naturally to her? What is she doing when she is deeply absorbed in a task of her own choosing? Do you value these qualities?

You may or may not value your child's strengths or talents because of your personal preferences. But your criticism of them will feel like a personal rejection to your youngster. Judi, a school principal, valued education and wanted her daughter Mary to value it too. But Mary excelled in sports, and she didn't spend the study time necessary to get straight A's. Her academic goal was only to get grades high enough to win an athletic scholarship.

Because Judi didn't value physical activity and could not see athletics as a proper profession for her daughter, tension, anger, and distance developed between them. Mary was made to feel that she was defective. Because of Judi's unwillingness to honor her daughter's talents, Mary dealt with her feelings of rejection by alienating herself from her mom. Both suffered the loss of a mother-daughter relationship. During therapy, Judi recognized the sadness she felt because of the strained relationship with her daughter. This was the first time she had allowed herself to be honest with her feelings in regard to her daughter. By appreciating Mary's happiness on the athletic field, she recognized her own stubbornness in focusing only on her own point of view.

Your job is to support your child as she develops her unique gifts and not divert her focus to your own agenda.

2. What is your child doing when you find yourself critical or angry with him? What is it you want him to be doing instead? How do you express your anger? Is any of the anger directed at him really meant for you?

As an adult you are responsible for expressing your feelings appropriately. If you repeatedly explode at your child for the same reasons, chances are you are triggering an unresolved issue from your own childhood that is causing you to criticize yourself. The resulting anger is easily projected onto your child.

3. What do you wish you could change about your child? Would you like to change anything about yourself?

Diane was continuously irate at her daughter because she was never ready to leave on time for scheduled activities. Yet tardiness was the very trait her boss had reprimanded Diane for. By yelling at her child to change her bad habits, Diane was subconsciously punishing herself.

4. What do you make sure to do for your child? Is this linked to your parents' insistence or are you compensating for a

deficit in your childhood home? How can you know if what you do is appropriate for your child?

Since you are such a busy person, it's probably difficult to do all that you would like to do with or for your child. How you choose to use your limited time will give you clues as to what is significant to you as a parent.

Sybil felt it important to be at home when her children returned from school. She wanted to sit with them and talk about the day's events. As a child, she had felt abandoned by her single mother, who seemed always to be working. Consequently, Sybil was a lonely and unhappy child.

Now that she had become a parent, being available for her children was her highest priority. Sybil's children, however, didn't want to talk with her right after school. They wanted to go out and play. The afternoons became scenes of power struggles between Sybil and her kids. This mother was parenting out of what she had needed when she was a child, not from what her children needed today. After completing this exercise, she was able to separate what she *thought* her children needed from what they *actually* needed.

5. What do you argue about with your child most frequently? Did you feel powerless about these issues as a child?

Powerlessness feels uncomfortable and diminishes one's self-image. If you were unable to get your way as a child, it is difficult to give in to what your child wants now. It may seem to you that relenting deprives you of influence or power once again. For example, when your child wants to spend the night at his friend's house, you may deny his request. If he fights for his point of view, your anger may escalate because he won't accept your authority. In one sense, you may be glad that your child has a stronger sense of self than you did, as demonstrated by his willingness to stand up for what he wants. But at the same time, you may feel enraged that you didn't have permission to express yourself when you were a child.

6. How do you feel when your child challenges you? Did you ever challenge your parents? What happened? How did that make you feel?

If you felt powerless in relation to your parents, you may believe it is important to feel in control as an adult. Unconsciously, you may feel that control protects you from ever feeling powerless again. Unfortunately, your need for control may make your child feel powerless, thus perpetuating the cycle. Later in this chapter you will see how to make decisions that empower both parent and child.

7. Objectively, how do you think and feel about your child?

Just as you may think positive thoughts about yourself but *feel* otherwise, you can experience a similar discrepancy in your perception of your child. Being aware of the differences in thoughts and feelings can help you understand why you're feeling conflicted about your child.

8. How is your child like you? How is your child different? Do you like or dislike the similarities and differences? Do you and your child compete in areas of similarity?

If you see similarities in you and your youngster, evaluate how you feel about them. If you don't like certain traits, be aware that they may be traits you reject in yourself. If you feel good about the similarities, remember they are only a part of your child. Don't think that your youngster is like you in all other ways. An over-generalization of similarities can prevent you from supporting your child's unique strengths; you may not even see them. Or you may pressure your youngster to participate in the same activities you do.

When you strive to be "number one" in relation to your child, you are competing with her. But beware. Any competition between you and your youngster occurs at the expense of her development. Children do not have the ability to compete with adults, nor should they be made to.

Again, just as in the previous guidelines, these questions are designed to help you to examine the parent-child relationship from a new perspective. Once you become aware of them, you can consciously choose to change patterns of interaction and behavior that may cause your youngster to underachieve.

Developing a Joint Vision

Your child needs to develop trust in interpreting his own life experiences. He does this when you allow him to summarize and draw conclusions about his experience. However, your child is influenced by your responses to what he says and does. Without realizing it, you may influence his perceptions with your own life experiences. This may prevent him from trusting that his experiences and his interpretation of them are valid. If a youngster cannot trust his own experiences to be his guide in making decisions, how will he become sufficiently self-confident to take the normal risks in life? What base will he have to support himself in new endeavors?

Underachieving children often can't trust themselves to know what is right for them. They may become increasingly dependent on others for direction, even as they rebel or reject this guidance. They may feel they don't know where to turn for answers.

As parents we have to help our children understand and interpret their life experiences without the overlay of our perceptions. Only after they express what an incident means to them should we help them expand their point of view, if necessary.

Sarah, age 13, loved to sing. She asked her mom, Linda, for voice lessons. Linda thought it an appropriate afterschool activity and promptly set up the lessons. Sarah's voice teacher appreciated the adolescent's talents. She suggested Sarah take private lessons and join a choir.

At first, Linda was concerned that all of these music activities would interfere with Sarah's schoolwork, but Sarah pleaded and promised she would keep up her grades, so Linda relented. School was easy for Sarah but she really didn't like it; all she loved was singing. Indeed, unbeknownst to her mother, Sarah had visions of becoming an opera or rock star.

When the Christmas show tryouts were announced, Sarah was sure she would get a major solo. After all, her teacher had told her she was very talented. When she landed only a minor part, Sarah was devastated. She came home crying.

Linda said, "Sarah, it's only voice lessons! Your grades are the important thing, and look at how good they are! Dry your eyes and stop being silly. This is not the end of the world!"

Unfortunately, to Sarah it was the end of the world. This was the first time she had really wanted to reach a goal and had been willing to try her hardest. The experience shook her confidence in herself. It also alienated her from her mother because Linda didn't understand what singing meant to her. Sarah now believed that she lacked the talent to follow her dreams. The joy went out of her life, and she quit singing.

A year after this incident, I met Sarah and Linda when they came for therapy. Sarah had withdrawn from life. They fought frequently about Sarah's negative attitude.

"What was happening in Sarah's life right before the depression started?" I inquired. Linda couldn't think of anything special. But I noticed Sarah looking up at me for the first time since she had come into the office. I asked her, "Do you want to tell me what happened a year ago?" She started to speak but then looked at her mom and shook her head no. So I told Linda, "I want to get to know Sarah a little better. Would you mind sitting in the reception room for a few minutes?"

When Sarah and I were alone, she started crying immediately. She related the sad tale of the audition and her mother's reaction to her tears. After this discussion, I could see how discounted Sarah felt. The audition had meant the world to her but had little value for her mom. But most unfortunately, Sarah was angry with herself for "being so stupid to think I could ever be a singer." When I asked Sarah how she felt when she sang, she replied with a broad grin, "Like a songbird."

Later when I met with Linda, I helped her see that singing was an important activity to Sarah. It motivated her to try her hardest in a way she never had before. Whether Sarah would become a professional singer was beside the point.

Linda had failed to ask Sarah, "How does this make you feel?" when the incident first occurred. Had she explored the significance of this disappointment with Sarah, she could have helped her daughter put it in perspective. She might have shown Sarah the value of participating, even with a minor solo, for the sheer pleasure of it. But most important, Linda should have regarded the singing as valuable because of its significance to her daughter. Finally, Linda could have noted to Sarah how happy she seemed when taking voice lessons. Such feedback helps children better understand their own experiences.

Linda offered to pay for singing lessons again and Sarah eagerly accepted. "This time I'm going to stick with it and not let disappointment railroad me. I want to see what I can do," exclaimed Sarah.

By using the guidelines for effective communication in chapter 7 to listen attentively and respond openly, you support your child in expressing her thoughts and feelings. That helps her personalize and interpret her own experiences. You and your youngster can then better appreciate her unique strengths and talents. When you recognize your agenda and values and separate them from your child's specialness, power struggles will diminish.

Establish and Reinforce House Rules

A power struggle is an arbitrary, emotional reaction to your child's behavior. It is an emotional tug-of-war that hides the real issues (such as independence, privileges, and responsibilities), leaving both parties confused and the issues unresolved. Disciplining your child, on the other hand, is a clear unemotional statement that defines the problem, the solution, and the consequences that will be taken if the solution is not implemented.

During a power struggle, parents often exert their authority to end the fight without resolving the underlying issues. Statements such as:

- "If you expect to ever use the phone again, you'll do it!"

- "Go to your room."

- "Do it because I say so or else."

are ineffectual in ending power struggles because they can intensify problems between parent and child. Now the child focuses on her resentment of your power, and you feel guilty for losing control. Indeed, you may give in because of your guilt, which further clouds the issues. Eventually your child may lose track of what is acceptable to you.

Spelling out consequences to the child in advance lessens the likelihood of power struggles. House rules make children feel safe; they know what is expected of them and what will happen if they don't follow through. By being consistent with these standards, you help your child understand the relationship between cause and effect, a key factor in developing a sense of responsibility. Examples of specified consequences and privileges include:

- "If your homework is done by 6:00 P.M. you may have phone privileges. If not, you may not use the phone for a 24-hour period."

- "If you maintain a B average you have the privilege of using the car. If not, you may not drive it until you raise your grades."
- "If you do your assigned chores you may go on outings with your friends on weekends. If not, you may not go out until the chores are done."

When your youngster experiences consequences and privileges, it becomes obvious to him that he, and no one else, is making things happen in his life. When children make this connection they develop a sense of power and responsibility.

Agreeing on Privileges Without Leaving Bodies on the Battlefield

Nothing gets power struggles going faster than a child who wants to be able to do something and a parent who refuses permission. Children constantly push their limits for more freedom and privileges. How do you decide what is appropriate?

All too often parents rely on their own life experience to determine if their child is ready to go to a Saturday afternoon movie with a friend, start dating, drive with friends, and the multitude of other milestones that arise as kids grow up. Yet, since children are individuals, they mature at different rates. You may have been responsible at age 12 but perhaps your child is not.

Being objective about your youngster helps you make the difficult decisions about privileges. How your child follows through with his responsibilities is the key factor in granting additional freedom. When I explain this concept to my clients, I use a simple equation: responsibility = privileges. I have the family take a piece of paper and list all of the child's responsibilities on one side and all his privileges on the other. We explore to see how consistently he fulfills his responsibilities and to determine if the privileges are balanced in turn. For example, if a child is consistently irresponsible in doing his chores, then he will probably not act responsibly at a theater with his friends. Only when you can see your child following through with his responsibilities can you expect him to act responsibly with new privileges. This formula prevents kids from hooking you emotionally, because you now are using facts to make your decisions.

Children are masters at making parents feel guilty, especially if "Johnny's mom is letting him go!" In this case, I always tell parents to check with the other parent; as you know, kids do exaggerate in the hope of getting their way.

Guilt seems to work especially well on overachieving parents of underachieving children. It's not often that underachievers show enthusiasm and determination. Since they seem to want a privilege so much, parents tend to give in because they know their kids are depressed, unhappy, or angry most of the time due to their many failures. But as you look at this situation objectively, you can see that giving in is the least effective way to support your underachiever. He becomes manipulative rather than grasping the cause-and-effect relationship between his behavior and his privileges.

By letting your child know that privileges will be granted based on his demonstrated responsibility, decision-making is no longer fraught with guilt and manipulation. It is clearly based on reason.

Erica, 13, and her family had been in counseling for four months. Her parents, Christy and Ken, quickly picked up the guidelines for effective communication and this helped them understand and work with Erica to change her belligerent attitude and poor grades. Erica was doing well. She responded to the homework and discipline accountability system and became more responsible for herself. She also knew about the responsibility = privileges equation.

Erica requested that her parents allow her to go to the mall with her girlfriends on Friday night without a chaperon. Both parents were startled since they had never allowed their daughter to go to the mall during the evening without one of them. When they mentioned this, Erica reminded them, "Well, you restricted my activities for the past year because of my attitude."

While this was an exaggeration, it was true that she had not been granted any new privileges in a long time. Before coming to counseling they had been so fed up with her attitude and behavior that new privileges were out of the question. But now that Erica was making progress, it was time to give her a little leeway.

I asked Erica's parents, "What do you feel comfortable with?" Christy replied, "I would agree to Erica going to the mall in the evening if I was at the mall. But I won't let her go alone with her friends." Needless to say, Erica objected strongly.

I suggested, "Let's fold a paper lengthwise and write Erica's responsibilities on one side and privileges on the other." Following my lead, Erica and her parents worked together to list her duties during the past month. Erica had been remiss in finishing her chores on time and had received consequences for her tardiness, but she had been consistently responsible about her homework. She had no missing assignments for the whole month. When Christy and Ken acknowledged Erica's wonderful accomplishments (especially in comparison to previous years), they agreed to reopen the discussion about the mall.

When you give your kids a privilege, it's important to reinforce their positive behavior by specifically stating what responsibilities they followed through with. Going to the mall and acting responsible within the limits her parents had set provided Erica another opportunity to demonstrate her growing maturity.

The family decided that the first time Erica went to the mall at night it would be with a girlfriend for a short period of time. Christy would drop her off, and two hours later her friend's mother would pick them up. They were to be standing outside the mall at a specified time and place. If things went as planned, Erica would be allowed to stay longer the next time. Parents and child each felt as if they had won.

Power struggles can be avoided when you are clear about what the situation means to both of you. This is accomplished through understanding and communicating your own thoughts and feelings about the situation and listening to your child's.

Use Teamwork to Resolve Differences of Opinion

When you become aware that a power struggle is gathering steam, it's best to immediately state your perception and decide whether the issues are most appropriately discussed at the moment. A simple, "We have a difference of opinion and we're getting upset because we are not taking the time to listen to each other," cuts the emotion and allows you to set up a family meeting (see chapter 6) or give each other the attention required to resolve differences.

Listen attentively to what your youngster says, and reflect her statement back to her to check for understanding. This kind of communication prevents power struggles from starting. Nothing can be resolved until you and your child express the issue fully. This discussion allows both of you to develop your thoughts and feelings about the subject and to clarify what you think you heard the other say. When your child listens attentively and repeats what she has heard, you can check on her understanding. This is especially useful when your youngster is emotionally invested in a certain outcome. Under those circumstances, she usually hears only what she wants or the portion of your statement with which she disagrees.

When Julia and her mom, Clare, came in for therapy, Julia refused to talk. In fact, she kept making faces as her mother spoke. When I asked Julia, "Would you like to express verbally what you're expressing nonverbally?" she started yelling.

"I never get anything I want," she shouted at her mother. I asked for some details and the problem emerged.

Julia and Clare had been arguing about an acceptable dress for Julia's junior prom. Julia was campaigning for a strapless number but her mother said, "No way!"

"All my friends have strapless dresses," Julia shouted. "It's just no big deal! Why do you always have to ruin everything! You probably want me to look like you! A nerd!"

Clare reacted to the overgeneralization and name-calling with some threats of her own. "Well, I won't let you go at all, if you don't watch your mouth."

When Julia shot back, "I don't care!" Clare felt obligated to exert her authority. "I won't accept being talked to like that," she declared. "You can't go to the prom and that's final!"

When I asked each to tell me how she felt, both admitted to feeling shaken and upset. Neither wanted to be backed into a corner, but that's exactly what had happened. After discussing the incident, I suggested they try a new approach. "First let's define the problem," I said. "You can't solve a problem unless you both understand it. Julia, is this argument about the dress or about your desire to make your own choices? And, Clare, are you concerned about the strapless dress or are you afraid that Julia is getting out of control?"

Neither could readily define the problem. But as they took turns listening and reflecting back to each other, the real issue emerged. Clare remembered that the girls who wore strapless dresses at her proms were considered loose or "easy." She certainly didn't want anyone to think that of her daughter. As for Julia, wearing a strapless dress meant that she was growing up and making decisions by herself. The solution came down to finding a dress that Julia loved but that also met her mom's decency standard.

Once the issue was defined, the problem-solving could begin. Julia and Clare listed all the alternative solutions. They included:

- Shopping together.
- Allowing Julia to shop with friends. She could ask the store to hold several favorites and come back later with her mom.
- Having Clare describe her standards. If the dress Julia bought didn't meet them, she would return it without question.

They discussed the pros and cons of each possible solution. Finally they decided that Julia would shop with her friends. When she found the dress she loved, she would call Clare, who would come to the store to give final approval.

Power struggles are stopped by taking responsibility for one's feelings and being open and honest. It takes time and the commitment to work together to resolve differences. Below are some questions that you can use as guidelines when you begin discussing solutions. This list is for both you and your child.

Talking Instead of Struggling

1. Listen carefully with all your attention. What did you hear the other person say? In your own words, repeat back what you heard.

2. What did you hear yourself saying?

3. How do you think the other person feels? Ask him if that is how he is feeling.

4. How do you feel?

5. What does the other person want?

6. What would you like from the other person?

7. What do you both agree on?

8. What specifically do you disagree on?

9. Ask the other person if she is ready to work on solving the problem. If not, ask what more she wants to say before solving the problem.

Resolving Differences—A Step-by-Step Method

Now that the feelings and thoughts are out in the open, it's time to move toward resolution. Again, these questions are for both you and your child.

1. Define the problem
   - What are you deciding?
   - Whose problem is this?
   - What part of the problem is your responsibility?
   - Who is involved in this decision?
2. List all the possible alternatives
   - How many solutions can you think of?
   - What would others do?
   - Do you already know something that could help you think of the situation another way?
3. Predict the consequences of each alternative
   - What will happen if you choose each of the alternatives?
   - Will the consequences be good for you?
   - Will the consequences be good for others?
4. Think of what is most important to you
   - How do you feel about it?
   - What do you think about it?
5. Make a decision
   - Does your choice feel right?

No one wins when there is a power struggle, but both parent and child win when you take the time to go through this process. Not only do you reach a compromise but you create respect and trust between you.

Chapter Ten

The Joy of the Journey

chieving parents value accomplishment. Having something tangible to show for their efforts proves that they have reached their goals. But for underachievers, an accomplishment simply represents another opportunity to be judged and found wanting. Either they produce and their parents love them, or they fail and their parents reject them again.

The pressure to perform is stressful indeed. As we have seen, overemphasis on the end product—achievement—is at the root of underachieving behaviors.

You can shift your emphasis from product to process. Once your child begins to see each step of the *process* of achievement as a mini-goal, she will not only be able to complete the task, but the quality of the end product will vastly improve. The key is to use your newly acquired communication and task analysis skills and your newfound ability to prevent power struggles to help your child recognize the satisfaction that comes from taking small steps toward her goals.

Product vs. Process

Sonja, age 10, was assigned to write a five-page report on a state in the union. She had two months to complete the assignment. Sonja, however, couldn't deal with writing five pages of anything, and her anxiety soared. To relieve the tension, she hid the assignment sheet in the back of her desk drawer. If she didn't have to look at it, she believed she wouldn't worry about it. Sonja's mother, Emily, found out about the report from the mother of Sonja's friend during a parent-teacher luncheon.

In a therapy session, Emily recounted how she handled the situation. When she confronted Sonja asking why she hadn't told her about the assignment two weeks earlier, Sonja froze in terror. All she could think about was the perfect example the teacher had shown the students in class. "I know I can never do the same," she told her mother. "I can't draw the way that student did or write as neatly. No matter how hard I try, my report will never be good enough for my teacher or you. It gives me a stomachache because I know I'm going to get another D and a lecture from you about how I should have done the report."

Sonja's automatic assumption that she couldn't do the assignment is a symptom of a habitual underachiever's hopelessness and helplessness. Her fear of risking the task (and failing) was out of proportion to the task itself. Sonja's self-defeating attitude becomes more ingrained each time an underachiever criticizes herself or is criticized by authority figures. But there is a solution.

As Emily listened to her daughter, she felt herself getting angry. She was tired of hearing rationalizations from her daughter, especially now since they had been doing so well in counseling. But she remembered to breathe deeply to control her anger. That allowed her to hear her daughter. By the time Sonja was finished telling Emily how she felt, it was obvious to this mother how they needed to proceed.

Emily recognized that Sonja needed specific skills to write the report—skills she didn't possess. She also recognized that Sonja would need support throughout the project, since the process of taking small steps to reach a larger goal was still foreign to her.

First, mother and daughter analyzed the tasks required to write the report. Sonja's first job was to go to the school library and bring home three books about Vermont. Emily then asked her daughter questions designed to build self-confidence by helping Sonja interpret her experience:

- "How did you decide on Vermont?"
- "Did you have any difficulty finding the books?"
- "How do you feel now that you completed step one?"

Sonja loved receiving positive attention from her mother. The fact that Emily cared enough to ask her questions and then listen to the answers validated her reality. As Sonja left the kitchen, she turned and said with a smile, "Maybe this report won't be as hard as I thought."

Acknowledging your child's emotions and efforts will help her feel good about herself. Acknowledgment means listening attentively and responding with statements that reinforce the appropriate behavior. Emily told Sonja the following day that she saw how hard she was working on taking notes from a reference book.

Each time your child completes one of the many steps toward reaching a goal, she learns something new about herself. Sonja learned that once she took the first step, her helplessness disappeared. Without fears to preoccupy her, she was able to put her full attention and effort into the task. That enabled her to enjoy doing her work. Once a child starts experiencing success in these small ways, she'll feel confident enough to begin changing her habitual thinking and feeling patterns.

When Children Take Failure to Heart

People tend to react to failure by judging themselves as inadequate and inferior. This leads to feelings of discouragement, which can easily dissolve into the abandonment of goals. While it is necessary to allow your child to feel and acknowledge the emotions associated with failure, it is equally important to prevent him from becoming frozen in them.

Failure can provide a wonderful opportunity to learn from experience. While achieving parents have learned how to derive meaning from disappointment and failure in their own lives, they are often highly critical of their children's failures.

Achieving parents have difficulty accepting failure as a necessary and important part of their youngster's growth. When the child performs poorly they overreact, fearing that if they remain complacent, failure will become a regular pattern. As a result, they express negative attitudes toward their children when they fail. But kids cannot distinguish between statements that criticize their behaviors from those that criticize their personhood. As a result, negative comments reduce a child's confidence and undermine his self-esteem. In truth, however, failure does not imply a defective character. It is simply the consequence of unrealistic goals and/or deficient skills.

In order to help your child view failure as a learning opportunity rather than an indictment, you must become aware of your emotional reaction when your child disappoints you. Do you feel guilty, as if *you* have failed? Do you get angry at yourself or you child? Observe your feelings about yourself and your child. Negative comments are self-defeating. They make you feel responsible for your child's failure and they reinforce his sense of hopelessness and helplessness. When your child associates criticism with failure, he predicts future performance from this conclusion. Underachievers tend to see options in black or white—either they succeed or they fail:

- Mike tried softball. Because he didn't make pitcher right away, he quit. "I'm a failure," he said.

- Cindy dreamed of being a cheerleader. She tried out in junior high and didn't make it. She refused to audition in high school. "There's no point," she said. "I'll never make it."

- When Megan didn't get into an honors science class, she judged herself a failure. She decided to abandon a medical career. "Why bother?" she asked.

When underachieving children fail at one goal, they doubt their abilities in other areas. Mike assumed that because he struck out as a softball pitcher, he wouldn't make it in other sports either. Cindy not only felt like a washout as a cheerleader, but she was also certain she would have trouble making friends. Because Megan believed she was a terrible student, she worried that she would be all thumbs at her new job too.

To compound the situation, underachievers have difficulty putting their shortcomings into perspective. As an adult, you can accept that you are mediocre at some tasks. You know that you're a great lawyer, so if you can't sing or play tennis, you still feel competent. Underachievers lack the ability to accept their weaknesses because they don't know their strengths. Their unrealistic picture of themselves makes them more sensitive to their failures than are children who achieve. But setbacks don't have to scar children or limit the goals they set for themselves.

Helping your child to learn from experience is the healthy way to deal with failure. A simple "What can we learn from this situation?" removes judgment and focuses you and your child on reviewing the situation. Failure becomes the teacher. And if parents and educators don't teach children to appreciate failure as a learning opportunity, kids feel worthless day after day.

When I asked a fifth-grader, Candy, to list all the times she felt like a failure in a given day, she presented me with the following:

- I forgot to empty the dishwasher before going to bed. My mom shouted, "Do I always have to remind you of everything? Can't you remember anything?"

- My teacher didn't believe that I didn't understand the last few math homework problems. She said I was irresponsible for not asking questions in class.

- At lunch, my best friend accused me of breaking my promise and telling everyone she liked Patrick. I only told Melinda because I thought I could trust her. Now no one in my group will talk to me.

- I didn't finish my apron in time to earn my sewing merit badge. All I had to do was attach the waistband to the gathered front part. When I asked the Girl Scout leader to show me how, she started yelling at me that it was too crooked. She said I had to do it over again. I was the only girl in my troop who didn't earn the badge.

- My teacher called my father and told him I was failing math. When he got off the phone Dad was furious. He said, "Well, what do you have to say for yourself? Why didn't you tell me you were failing? Do you know how embarrassing it is for the family to have a teacher call? Your sister never has the teacher calling! I want to see you doing math homework every night! Now go up to bed and think about how you are going to get a better grade!"

As Candy experienced her day, each sense of failure added to her erroneous conclusion that she could do nothing right. But as we worked in therapy, Candy's parents came to understand how their judgmental attitude toward their daughter's performance caused her to lie habitually. The child hoped to cover up her shortcomings so she wouldn't have to endure her parents' condemning lectures. She even tried to deny her failures to herself because they were so painful.

In the course of family therapy, Candy and her family learned to appreciate failure as an opportunity for learning and growth. With her parents' support, Candy was able to accept and learn from her experiences. She realized that she had lost sight of the due date for her apron, so she bought a large calendar to mark important future dates. She resolved to ask questions during math lessons and then request additional help from her teacher after school. She hung a sign on her mirror reminding her to empty the dishwasher before going to bed. And she apologized to her chum for betraying a confidence and asked for another chance to be her friend. Since the family was communicating effectively without criticism, Candy no longer needed to lie.

Underachievers cannot tolerate failure if it is associated with criticism:

- The excuse-maker will blame the failure on someone or something else.
- The master manipulator will make it seem as if she is a victim of the situation.
- The dropout will use failure as a justification to leave the system.
- The people-pleaser will experience anxiety and shame.
- The procrastinator will use failure to justify putting off her work for fear she can't do it.

All underachievers try to cover up their weaknesses. Their shortcomings indicate to these youngsters that they are also failures as *people*. And that's a conclusion too devastating to deal with.

How to Turn Failure into an Opportunity for Growth

Al and Maria brought their 11-year-old Richard in for counseling because they were disgusted with his school performance. Each year Richard promised to try harder but the promised A's never materialized. This would set off the never-ending battle between Al and Richard, a battle filled with accusations and recriminations. On the one hand Richard wanted to get good grades. He hoped that each new year would bring different results. But on the other, Richard felt like an impostor. He feared he could never achieve to his father's standards. His expectations of his own failure were too powerful to overcome.

When I asked Richard during family therapy what it was like to bring home poor grades, he cried, "I'm afraid of my father's yelling. He hates me, I hate school. I hate myself. I'm stupid. Why doesn't everyone leave me alone?"

"There you go again," replied Al. "All you want is sympathy. If you would just be responsible, then you won't be a failure!" Father and son were caught up with criticizing Richard's performance.

I asked Richard and his parents to accept the boy's failures as the result of still unknown causes and not as a personal statement about him or his value. Then I turned to Richard and asked, "Are you willing to look at the whole situation and see what we can learn from your repeating patterns?" He nodded. "Tell me, Richard, what do you think about the situation?"

The boy's circular reasoning became obvious in his reply: "I feel stupid when I don't understand what the teacher is saying, but I'm afraid to ask questions because then the teacher might find out I'm stupid. So I just draw pictures in class." No wonder Richard was going nowhere fast.

After doing a task analysis of his work, study, and organizational skills, we found that Richard had to develop seven skills in order to reach his goals. In addition, we agreed we wouldn't wait for the end of the grade reporting period to see if his skills were improving. We asked the teacher for more frequent feedback.

Each week we set two goals for Richard, one applying a skill he had learned the previous week, and the other a new skill to be mastered. Each Friday his teacher used a form we designed to give Richard feedback on how she saw him applying the skills of the week. Then Maria and Al would sit down with their son and ask him if he saw a difference in his work. They wanted to know how he felt about it. These talks make Richard feel more self-confident about his ability to assess his own behavior. And each week Richard received supportive, nonjudgmental acknowledgment, which motivated him to continue working. At the end of the reporting period, he had met all of his goals, thus greatly enhancing his sense of worth. He even started to enjoy doing his work, further evidence of his new attitude toward himself and his responsibilities.

Underachieving children feel defeated before they ever attack a goal because they feel overwhelmed by their expectation of failure. Not only are they unable to understand the individual tasks involved, but they don't know how to support themselves or gain the support of others to sustain their effort in the long haul. Their preoccupation with having to accomplish the goal undermines their ability to pace themselves and break the tasks into manageable steps. They fear that a new project represents yet another opportunity to disappoint themselves and their parents. Turning failure into a learning process that will automatically bring achievement alleviates its paralyzing emotional impact.

Changing Failure into a Learning Experience

The following guide will help you transform failure into a learning process. As with all of the guidelines in this book, you will need to call upon the skills involved in communication, task analysis, and prevention of power struggles to support your child through this often painful process.

1. *Allow your child to express his feelings about the situation.* He needs to verbalize the emotional pain associated with failure in order to allow the bottled-up emotions to escape. Your job is to be an attentive listener. When you reflect back what you heard, you validate his experience.

2. *Support your child in accepting the situation without self-criticism.* Once your youngster expresses her feelings, help her feel safe to admit she did make mistakes and needs to do things differently. Rather than criticizing her failure, express your willingness to work together to figure out what can be done to correct the situation. A simple statement such as, "Let's work this out together," reassures your child that you won't criticize her.

3. *Assist your child in analyzing the facts.* Use questions to help your youngster clarify the situation. It's essential to define the problem from your child's point of view. Next perform a task analysis for each issue to help your child recognize what he can do to resolve the problem. (The task analysis questions in chapter 8 would be helpful at this point.)

4. *Develop a plan with your child to resolve the problems.* When you review all the tasks that your youngster needs to learn and apply, you're ready to help her decide on the priorities, time limits, responsibilities, and (if appropriate) consequences, privileges, and rewards. Assemble the plan step by step. This process helps underachievers help themselves. Start slowly to ensure that she sees that her new behavior makes a difference.

5. *Together, decide on the first step and support your child in going for it.* Make the first step easy, specific, and measurable. No matter how small the step, be sure you ask your child how he feels about accomplishing it. Acknowledge the completion of the task.

6. *Support your child in checking his feelings along the way.* Asking your child about his feelings supports him in learning about them and changing them. Since underachievers expect to disappoint themselves and their parents, they naturally associate trying anything new with negative feelings. They have not yet learned to connect positive feelings with new behaviors. So as your youngster launches into new behaviors (and sees them work), he will need to identify his feelings and the new relationship between his behaviors and emotions. When you ask your child how he feels after he has accomplished an early step in his plan, don't be surprised if he says, "Okay." When you feel it is appropriate, you might ask him to give you a feeling word that helps you understand what he means by "okay."

7. *Review the plan with your child to help her internalize her success.* Listening to your child as she recounts her story of success is an important way to support her in affirming herself. When she has the opportunity to talk about her doubts along the journey and recognize her ability to move through them, it solidifies her positive experience. In effect, she is updating her self-image. Once children see that failure will not bring criticism, they have an easier time trying new goals.

Dealing with Discouragement, Frustration, and Anger Along the Way

Discouragement, frustration, and anger are all too familiar to underachievers. Discouragement is caused by a lack of confidence in one's ability, frustration is caused by not knowing how to do a task, and anger is hostility toward the task and one's self. When children are in the grip of these emotions, their rational thinking shuts down and they become unable to complete the task. Indeed, they often become confused about their emotional state: they don't know what caused it or what to do about it.

Steve, age nine, was doing his math homework at the kitchen table while his mother was making dinner. Angie heard her son erasing often and sensed how stressed he was becoming. But since she knew he would yell at her to leave him alone if she interfered, she left the room.

Steve tried to do the next division problem by himself but couldn't remember where to put the number in the quotient. He demonstrated his frustration by crumpling his paper. Seeing the wadded-up homework and realizing he would have to redo what he had already done, Steve felt overwhelmed by his sense of inadequacy and his negative feelings toward himself, math, his teacher, and school in general. By globalizing his frustration from the one math problem to his whole life, Steve became enraged. Because this buildup of emotion was uncomfortable, he released it by hitting his two-year-old sister on the arm as she walked into the kitchen. Hearing her daughter cry, Angie ran into the kitchen to find out what had happened. She yelled at Steve, who now felt even worse but didn't understand the cause of his frustration and anger. Again needing a way to vent his escalating anger, he talked back to Angie, creating further problems. The real cause of the anger was never identified and the math homework was forgotten in the emotional turmoil that followed.

Negative feelings progress in intensity if they are not resolved. Most commonly, discouragement moves to frustration and on to anger. Steve relieved his anger by being aggressive with his sister. However, many children stifle their anger and withdraw into depression or an escapist activity such as watching television or playing video games.

This negative emotional cycle prevents youngsters from paying attention to the task at hand. Once the project is given up, the child again perceives that he can't complete anything. Another failure!

Helping your child identify and understand the causes of his feelings can prevent him from being sabotaged by them. I helped

Steve understand the effect his negative feelings had on his ability to finish the task. I asked, "Tell me, Steve, what were you doing right before you hit your sister? How were you feeling?"

"I wadded up my paper. I was fed up, frustrated, and angry. I was ready to explode," replied Steve.

This helped him see the relationship between his feelings of frustration, discouragement, and anger and the inappropriate way he vented them. Then I asked him, "How did you feel about the math and about yourself while you were trying to do your homework?"

"I wadded up the paper because I was mad that I couldn't do it. I hate the stupid book for being so hard!" he replied.

"Were you also angry at yourself because you couldn't do the math?" I asked.

After taking a moment to think about it, he said, "Yes." Steve recognized that his inability to do the work triggered his frustration. He was angry at his sense of inadequacy as a person. He had felt frustrated so many times. He then realized he had expressed his anger at his sister because he hadn't known the cause of it.

Children need to ask for help before their sense of discouragement grows into frustration and anger. It's essential to talk with your child so he can recognize how he behaves when he feels discouraged. Some kids may use any excuse to stop working, such as going to the bathroom unnecessarily or getting something to eat. Others become frustrated and angry immediately and express those feelings inappropriately. They can be irritable or they may bait a parent or sibling into starting a fight.

If your child can't identify how he shows these emotions, then it's appropriate to give him feedback. Tell him what you observe when he's in the throes of these negative feelings. A statement like, "Max, when you're angry you pick on your brother for no reason," helps him connect his behavior with his emotions.

Once your child recognizes his feelings, he can do something about them. If Steve could have said, "This is hard. I'm getting discouraged," that might have prevented him from becoming critical of himself and the situation. The first sign of frustration should have been Steve's clue to ask for help. The aim of this awareness is not to prevent the discouragement; like any feeling, it is a signal for you and your child to assess the situation. Rather, the aim is to help your child take appropriate action to deal with the cause of the emotion. Feelings don't have to be saboteurs. They can be helpful friends when we understand what they mean.

Making the Journey an Adventure: Transforming Negatives into Positives

The repetition of negative thoughts and feelings can paralyze underachievers. But change is possible using a three-step process:

1. Help your child become aware of her self-critical thoughts and feelings. Ask her to write down her negative self-talk after she has disappointed herself or others. Explain how her thoughts influence her behavior. As I told one young client, "If you think you are stupid, then you'll give up the first time you're unsure of yourself. Self-criticism reinforces bad feelings about yourself."

2. Encourage your child to change these thoughts to more empowering statements, such as, "I can do it!" "I accept myself," and "I am smart." These positive statements give the child confidence and direction.

3. Help your child notice and appreciate all the times he succeeds at a new task. Encourage him to give himself credit for such accomplishment.

Lola was too shy to get up in front of the class. "I'm afraid I won't be able to remember what I want to say, and then the kids in my class will laugh at me," she worried during a therapy session.

But Lola was willing to substitute a more empowering thought whenever she felt concerned about an upcoming speech. Her new self-talk: "I feel confident to talk in front of a group because I am well prepared, and I know what I want to say." After correcting her faulty thinking, Lola was willing to risk giving her oral report. She also knew that no matter what actually transpired, she would learn from the experience.

During the next therapy session, Lola was eager to relate the result of our little experiment. The fact that she actually stood up in front of the class had a great influence on her thinking. She had proved to herself that she could do it. I asked what her new thought was about herself. She replied, "I can easily speak in front of any group."

Emotions can limit us or motivate us to experience life fully. They can energize us or sap our vitality. Inquiring of your child how she feels about herself or about events models what she needs to do internally. Asking her to tell you what she does when she's depressed, angry, or sad helps her identify the behaviors associated with each emotion. You might suggest that she keep a daily journal to help her be aware of her feelings. Instruct her to jot down the most important things that happened that day and then describe how she felt about them. This exercise can yield valuable insights. You may also suggest to your child that she ask herself how she is feeling at least three times a day. This will help her make a habit of being in touch with her emotions.

Annette had new hope that she was going to do well in school. She had learned a great deal from her academic failure the previous year. She now understood the importance of monitoring her thoughts and feelings so she could observe what made her self-critical. She knew she would have a better chance to reach her goals if she concentrated on affirming, confidence-building, empowering thoughts. To get herself in the habit of checking her emotions, she wrote the word "feelings" on her assignment sheet in large pink letters. In that way, every time she noted an assignment, she would also stop, assess her emotional state, and write it down at the moment. Also she created a statement for moments of discouragement: "I am confident that I can handle this situation. I know the right thing to do for me." Her positive and empowering affirmations gave her the self-confidence she needed to deal with challenging situations.

Together we designed a unique plan. As soon as she opened her eyes in the morning, Annette reached for personally decorated three-by-five cards upon which she had written her own positive statements. One such statement was, "I have everything I need to get everything I want. Today is going to be a wonderful day!" She repeated these affirmations and then visualized herself eager and confident to go to school. During the visualization, she made sure she felt enthusiastic, positive, and confident. Then she would get dressed in clothes she had laid out the night before. Being organized in the morning short-circuited frustrations about having "nothing to wear" that could start the day off on a negative note. At night she wrote in her journal, keeping her focused on her emotions and also improving her writing skills.

From her conscious effort to monitor thoughts and feelings, Annette started to feel more in control of her life. That gave her the confidence to change her behavior. She didn't hesitate to ask the teacher and other classmates for help if she was having a hard time doing her work. She paid attention in class and followed through with the new study methods she learned from her teacher. Her new behaviors then changed her self-image. Eventually, her expectations changed from failure to success.

Here are some questions and suggestions you can use to help your child gain a better awareness of his thoughts and feelings.

1. Ask your child to share what he's thinking when he feels down.

2. Help your child develop some empowering statements to use at those moments. Have your child say them aloud or to himself and then evaluate how he feels saying them. You may want to share an affirmation you use.

3. Help your child understand how negative feelings such as frustration, depression, anger, rejection, sadness, helplessness, and powerlessness impact her behavior. Point out the differences in her behavior when she feels empowering emotions such as happiness, enthusiasm, joy, and excitement.

4. Discuss ways that your child can get into the habit of evaluating her feelings.

5. Design with your child activities that she can do when she is feeling down or angry. (For example, she could express herself to you or a friend, write down her feelings in a journal, play music, or engage in a physical activity.)

Words to Encourage and Guide By

As underachievers practice new thoughts, feelings, and behaviors, they are likely to experience emotional ups and downs. It's human nature to resist change until we feel secure and comfortable in the new direction. Even if old behaviors are self-defeating, we cling to them because they are predictable. Since new behaviors are uncomfortable, they can produce insecurity—the feeling an underachiever tries to avoid at all costs. Insecurity feels too much like powerlessness and can cause the youngster to shut down and give up. During the transition, your child will need your support to keep him focused on adhering to new behaviors.

Encouraging statements show your faith in your child's abilities. You comment on specific behaviors that contribute to his eventual success. You must focus on your child's observable improvements and acknowledge his effort:

- "Kyle, when I read your paragraph on balloons, I was able to visualize them swaying in the wind. Your use of adverbs and adjectives made it easy for me to get a feel for the movement. Looks like you put a lot of thought into it."

- "Don, the way you cleaned your room is an improvement from last week. I noticed you put away all your clothes and straightened up your closet. I see you really put a great deal of effort into it."

Pinpointing your child's progress helps him understand which behaviors lead to success.

Encouraging statements also take into account your child's response to the situation. This is yet another way to show him your acceptance:

- "Burt, you seemed pleased that you got all your homework done, went to practice, and cleaned your room. I'm glad to see how well you managed your time."

- "Regina, you look excited about your teacher's comment on your paper. I'm glad you are enjoying doing your homework."

It's important to reflect your youngster's attitude in these statements because that helps her connect her positive feelings with her successful behaviors. Encouraging statements let your child know that you appreciate her progress without your hidden value judgment. These statements should be devoid of expectations for continued similar behavior. Let's look at two examples of well-intending parents who put criticism into what they thought were encouraging statements. Notice how these statements could be altered so that they support the child's progress.

Criticism:	"Wow, I'm so proud of you, you finally got an A on a math test! All you have to do is get an A on the next test, and you'll be able to bring up your grade."
Encouraging statement:	"I see you are pleased with yourself. Your hard work paid off, and you earned an A on your math test."
Criticism:	"Look what you can do when you try. I told you, you could do anything if you set your mind to it! It will be a breeze for you to win first place on your next science project!"
Encouraging statement:	"I saw you consistently working on your science project. I liked the way you followed through. How do you feel about getting an honorable mention?"

Your child becomes empowered when you reflect on his successes. Your encouragement shows respect for him and faith that he can choose to become successful.

You may need to practice formulating encouraging statements. The following are some situations in which parents have used encouragement to give hope and confidence to their children:

- Marla was in the habit of waiting until the last minute to do her long-term projects. But this time she wanted to get a jump on an assignment. She awakened early one Sunday to work on her Drug-Free Living poster. Her mother observed her working for three hours without interruption and later said, "I saw you working steadily for three hours. It looked like you were really working hard." With this statement Marla's mom was letting her know that she acknowledged her daughter's new attitude toward schoolwork. There were no recriminations about past disappointments or suggestions that Marla should continue in this vein now that she knew she could do it. With this nonjudgmental statement Marla was free to respond to her mother or just absorb her comment.

- Jake hated reading because it was hard for him. This caused him to turn in sloppy, illegible, incomplete work. Both his mother and teacher were now giving him additional help. As Jake's mother dropped off laundry in his room she noticed papers sitting on his school books. His handwriting had improved. Jake's mother commented, "I see that your handwriting is getting better. Before, I couldn't tell the difference between an 'i' or an 'e'. Now I can clearly see each letter."

- Carol was leaving the kitchen as her mom went in to get a drink of water. Her mother was pleasantly surprised to see the kitchen sparkle from Carol's efforts. "Carol, you have come a long way in cleaning the kitchen. I appreciate that you chose to do such a complete job. Thank you!"

- Gordon missed the baseball in a key play in Saturday's game. He was depressed and angry. "You may not feel very good about your baseball skills right now, son," said his father, "but look how much you have improved as a player since the beginning of the season."

Encouraging statements help your child maintain a perspective on daily events so that one misfortune doesn't affect his overall attitude about abilities. It was okay for Gordon to feel depressed about the game, but if he generalized that feeling to other areas, he would put himself in the underachieving thinking patterns.

Encouragement is a positive, nonjudgmental tool to empower your child. As he takes responsibility for dealing with his thoughts and feelings, as he works on each small step toward his goal, he will feel increasingly successful. These small successes will make him feel good about himself. And he will see that the journey is truly enjoyable because he has learned to handle any problems along the way. This new sense of confidence that he can make a difference in his own life provides the motivation and joy to seek ever-widening goals.

You and your child now have the tools to work in a new direction that will bring the success and happiness you want for your family. Working together, you can help your child become the magnificent person you both know he is!

Bibliography

Armstrong, Thomas. *In Their Own Way*. Los Angeles: Jeremy P. Tarcher.

Bandler, Richard; John Grinder; and Virginia Satir. *Changing with Families*. California: Science and Behavior.

Bradshaw, John. *Home Coming*. New York: Bantam.

Buzan, Tony. *Use Both Sides of Your Brain*. New York: E. P. Dutton.

Canter, Lee, with Marlene Canter. *Assertive Discipline*. Los Angeles: Canter and Associates.

Cavanaugh, Eunice. *Understanding Shame*. Minneapolis: Johnson Institute.

Dreikurs, Rudolph, and Vicki Stolz. *Children, the Challenge*. New York: Dutton.

Egan, Gerard. *The Skilled Helper*. California: Brooks/Cole.

Erikson, Erik H. *Childhood and Society*. New York: W. W. Norton.

Golant, Susan, and Mitch Golant. *Getting Through to Your Kids*. Los Angeles: Lowell House.

Guilford, J. P. *The Nature of Human Intelligence*. New York: McGraw-Hill.

Holt, J. *How Children Fail*. New York: Dell.

Jung, C. G. *The Archetypes and the Collective Unconscious*. New Jersey: Princeton University Press.

Keirsey, David, and Marilyn Bates. *Please Understand Me: An Essay on Temperament Styles*. California: Prometheus Nemesis.

Lawrence, Gordon. *People Types and Tiger Stripes.* Gainesville, Fla.: Center for Applications of Psychological Type.

Maslow, Abraham. *Farther Reaches of Human Nature.* New York: Viking Press (Esalen Series).

——. *Motivation and Personality.* New York: Harper and Row.

Miller, Alice. *The Drama of the Gifted Child.* New York: Basic Books.

Patterson, C. H. *Theories of Counseling and Psychotherapy.* New York: Harper and Row.

Pearce, Joseph Chilton. *Magical Child Matures.* New York: E. P. Dutton.

Piaget, Jean. *The Origins of Intelligence in Children.* New York: International Universities Press.

Restak, Richard, M. *The Mind.* New York: Bantam.

Satir, Virginia. *Conjoint Family Therapy.* California: Science and Behavior.

Torrance, E. Paul. *Education and the Creative Potential.* Minneapolis: University of Minnesota Press.

Whitfield, Charles L. *Healing the Child Within.* Pompano Beach, Fla.: Health Communications.

Index

LIBRARY
ST. LOUIS COMMUNITY COLLEGE
AT FLORISSANT VALLEY,